The ULTIMATE Book of CROSS STITCH

Jane Alford • Angela Beazley • Julie Hasler
Christina Marsh • Lynne Porter • Shirley Watts

INDEX

THE CHARTS

Some of the designs in this book are very detailed and, due to inevitable space limitations, the charts may be shown on a comparatively small scale; in such cases, readers may find it helpful to have the particular chart with which they are currently working enlarged.

THREADS

The projects in this book were all stitched with DMC, Anchor or Madeira stranded cotton embroidery threads. The keys given with each chart also list thread combinations for all three types of thread. It should be pointed out that the shades produced by different companies vary slightly, and it is not always possible to find identical colours in a different range.
Due to the difficulty of true photograph colour reproduction, the threads recommended do not always match the photographs exactly.

Published in 1997 by Merehurst Limited
Ferry House, 51-57 Lacy Road, Putney, London SW15 1PR

Text on pp 110-129 © Copyright Jane Alford 1997
Text on pp 46-49, 54-57, 66-69, 86-89, 98-101, 170-177 © Copyright Julie Hasler 1997
Text on pp 162-165, 178-181, 226-233, 238-245, 250-253 © Copyright Shirley Watts 1997
All other text © Copyright Merehurst Limited 1997
Photography and illustrations © Copyright Merehurst Limited 1997

ISBN 1-897730-41-1

A catalogue record for this book is available from the British Library.

Edited by Heather Dewhurst and Diana Lodge
Designed by Maggie Aldred
Photography by Marie-Louise Avery (all pages except pp 12-41, 46-47, 62-99, 162-163, 170-179, 186-187, 226-231, 238-243, 250-251); Debbie Patterson (pp 12-41); and Juliet Piddington (pp 46-47, 62-99, 162-163, 170-179, 186-187, 226-231, 238-243, 250-251)
Illustrations by John Hutchinson
Typesetting by Dacorum Type & Print, Hemel Hempstead
Printed in Hong Kong by MIDAS

Merehurst is the leading publisher of craft books and has an excellent range of titles to suit all levels. Please send to the address above for our free catalogue, stating the title of this book.

CONTENTS

INTRODUCTION

Cross stitch is one of the oldest, and simplest, of all embroidery stitches, and is part of embroidery heritage in countries all over the world. Cross stitch was often used to decorate household items such as linen and clothes, and is still used today for this purpose. However, with the tremendous revival of cross stitch in recent times, it is now possible to find a wide variety of products in which to mount your embroidery, including clothes brushes, glass coasters and trinket boxes.

The Ultimate Book of Cross Stitch is filled with a huge variety of cross stitch projects covering many favourite stitching themes: weddings, births, animals, alphabets, samplers, and country life. The wide range of projects, which cater for both the cross stitch novice and the seasoned stitcher, include cushions, pictures, frames, table linen, greetings cards and gifts for children.

The first chapter in the book, Wedding Celebrations, commemorates that most delightful of occasions with a range of gifts to stitch for the day and to serve as mementoes of the occasion.

The New Arrival is the title of the second chapter. This collection of designs includes many charming gifts to sew for a new baby, ranging from a cot cover to a decorated bib. Gifts for Children, the following chapter, caters for older children, and will solve all present-buying dilemmas for quite some time! You can make decorated school bags, toy bags, and even a wall chart.

The Chapter on Samplers provides some traditional designs on a traditional theme, such as a wedding sampler and a favourite 'Home Sweet Home' sampler, in addition to a few more contemporary ideas, such as the delightful farmyard sampler. The Alphabets chapter features a range of different cross stitch alphabet designs, including an amusing animal alphabet for children, which you can use to decorate and personalize clothes, samplers, pictures and gifts.

Quick and Easy Projects is the perfect chapter for those who love stitching but who don't have much spare time. With the designs in this book, you will be able to see the results of your stitching within a couple of hours.

Animals are an ever popular theme with stitchers and this chapter brings together some of the most delightful designs of farmyard animals and mischevious puppies. The final chapter is entitled Country Life and features several scenes of the countryside and its wildlife.

Cross stitch is a wonderfully easy stitch to learn and you do not require years of experience to produce very pleasing results. In this book, each design is carefully charted and colour coded and is accompanied by simple step-by-step instructions for making up the item.

Also included is a Basic Skills section, which covers everything from preparing your fabric and stretching it in an embroidery hoop or frame, to mounting your cross stitch embroidery ready for display. This ensures that, whatever your level of experience, you will be able to enjoy creating beautiful things for your, your friends and your family.

Happy Stitching!

BASIC SKILLS

·

BEFORE YOU BEGIN

PREPARING THE FABRIC

Even with an average amount of handling, many evenweave fabrics tend to fray at the edges, so it is a good idea to overcast the raw edges, using ordinary sewing thread, before you begin. Alternatively, wrap masking tape over the edges.

FABRIC

Some projects in this book use Aida fabric, which is ideal for beginners and more advanced stitchers as it has a surface of clearly designated squares. All Aida fabric has a count, which refers to the number of squares (each stitch covers one square) to 2.5cm (1in); the higher the count, the smaller the finished stitching.

Other projects in this book use either 14- or 18-count Aida, popular and readily available sizes, in a wide variety of colours. Linen has been used for several projects in this book; although less simple to stitch on than Aida fabric (because you need to count over a specified number of threads) it does give a very attractive, traditional finish. The most commonly available linen has 28 threads to 2.5cm (1in), which when worked over two threads gives a stitch count of 14 to 2.5cm (1in).

THE INSTRUCTIONS

Each project begins with a full list of the materials that you will require. Aida, Tula, Lugana and Linda are all fabrics produced by Zweigart. Note that the measurements given for the embroidery fabric include a minimum of 3cm (1¼in) all around to allow for stretching it in a frame and preparing the edges to prevent them from fraying.

Colour keys for stranded embroidery cottons – DMC, Anchor, or Madeira – are given with each chart. It is assumed that you will need to buy one skein of each colour mentioned in a particular key, even though you may use less, but where two or more skeins are needed, this information is included in the main list of requirements.

To work from the charts, particularly those where several symbols are used in close proximity, some readers may find it helpful to have the chart enlarged so that the squares and symbols can be seen more easily. Many photocopying services will do this for a minimum charge.

Before you begin to embroider, always mark the centre of the design with two lines of basting stitches, one vertical and one horizontal, running from edge to edge of the fabric, as indicated by the arrows on the charts.

As you are stitching, use the centre lines given on the chart and the basting threads on your fabric as reference points for counting the squares and threads so that you can position your design accurately on the fabric.

WORKING IN A HOOP

A hoop is the most popular frame for use with small areas of embroidery. It consists of two rings, one fitted inside the other; the outer ring usually has an adjustable screw attachment so that it can be tightened to hold the stretched fabric in place. Embroidery hoops are readily available in several sizes, ranging from 10cm (4in) in diameter to quilting hoops with a diameter of 38cm (15in). Hoops with table stands or floor stands attached are also available.

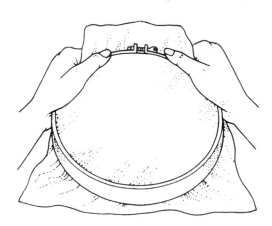

1 To stretch your fabric in a hoop, place the area to be embroidered over the inner ring and press the outer ring over it, with the tension screw released. Tissue paper can be placed between the outer ring and the embroidery, so that the hoop does not mark the fabric. Lay the tissue paper over the fabric when you set it in the hoop, then tear away the central embroidery area. If the fabric creases, release the outer hoop and try again.

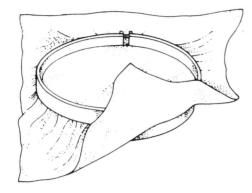

2 Smooth the fabric and, if necessary, straighten the grain before tightening the screw. The fabric should be evenly stretched.

EXTENDING EMBROIDERY FABRIC

It is easy to extend a piece of embroidery fabric, such as a bookmark, to stretch it in a hoop.

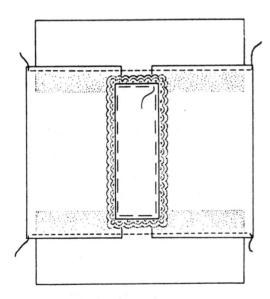

● Fabric oddments of a similar weight can be used. Simply cut four pieces to size (in other words, to the measurement that will fit both the embroidery fabric and your hoop) and baste them to each side of the embroidery fabric before stretching it in the hoop in the usual way.

WORKING IN A RECTANGULAR FRAME

Rectangular frames are more suitable for larger pieces of embroidery. They consist of two rollers, with tapes attached, and two flat side pieces, which slot into the rollers and are held in place by pegs or screw attachments. Available in different sizes, frames are measured by the length of the roller tape, ranging from 30cm (12in) to 68cm (27in).

As alternatives to a slate frame, canvas stretchers and the backs of old picture frames can be used. Provided there is sufficient extra fabric around the finished size of the embroidery, the edges of the fabric can be turned under and simply attached to the sides of the frame with drawing pins (thumb tacks) or staples.

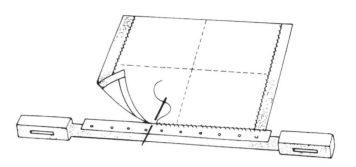

1 To stretch your fabric in a rectangular frame, cut out the fabric, allowing at least an extra 5cm (2in) all around the finished size of the embroidery. Baste a single 12mm (½in) turning on the top and bottom edges and oversew strong tape, 2.5cm (1in) wide, to the other two sides. Mark the centre line on the fabric both ways with large basting stitches. Working from the centre outwards and using a needle and strong thread, oversew the top and bottom edges to the roller tapes. Fit the side pieces into the slots, and roll any extra fabric on one roller until the fabric is completely taut.

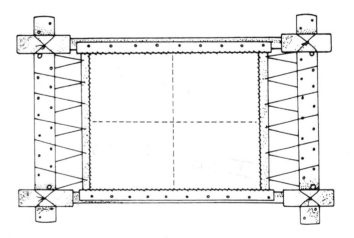

2 Insert the pegs or adjust the screw attachments to secure the frame. Thread a large-eyed needle (chenille needle) with strong thread or fine string and lace both edges of the fabric, securing the ends around the intersections of the frame. Lace the webbing at 2.5cm (1in) intervals, stretching the fabric evenly.

WORKING WITH WASTE CANVAS

Waste canvas has been used for some of the designs in this book. This canvas, quite simply, provides a removable grid over which you can stitch on unevenly-woven fabrics. Once the design has been stitched, the canvas is removed. Firstly, determine the size of the design, and cut a piece of canvas that allows a border of a least 5cm (2in) all around. Baste the waste canvas to the design area of the fabric/item you are using. Stitch your design in the usual way, making sure it is centred on the fabric/item. When stitching is complete, remove the basting stitches and lightly dampen the canvas with water. Slowly and gently pull out the threads of canvas, one at a time, using a pair of tweezers. Don't hurry this process, as it could result in spoiling your stitching. You may need to re-dampen stubborn threads that will not pull out.

THE STITCHES

CROSS STITCH

For all cross stitch embroidery, the following two methods of working are used. In each case, neat rows of vertical stitches are produced on the back of the fabric.

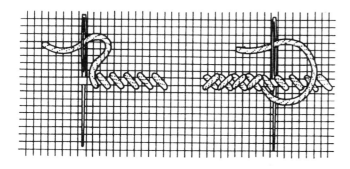

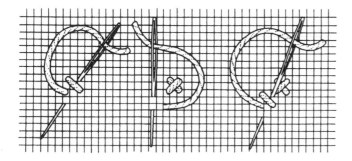

● When stitching large areas of one colour, such as a background, it is easiest to work in horizontal rows. Working from right to left, complete the first row of evenly spaced diagonal stitches over the number of threads specified in the project instructions. Then, working from left to right, repeat the process. Continue in this way to fill the area, following the chart, making sure each stitch crosses in the same direction.

● When stitching diagonal lines in a design, work downwards, completing each stitch before moving to the next. Make sure all the crosses look the same, with the top of the cross going in the same direction. When starting a project always begin to embroider at the centre of the design and work outwards to ensure that the design will be placed centrally on the fabric.

THREE-QUARTER CROSS STITCH

Some fractional stitches are used on certain projects in this book; although they strike fear into the hearts of less experienced stitchers they are not difficult to master, and give a more natural line in certain instances. Should you find it difficult to pierce the centre of the Aida block, simply use a sharp needle to make a small hole in the centre first, before making the stitch.

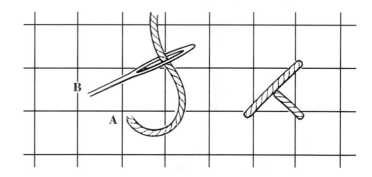

● To work a three-quarter cross, bring the needle up at point A and down through the centre of the square at B. Later, the diagonal back stitch finishes the stitch. A chart square with two different symbols separated by a diagonal line requires two 'three-quarter' stitches. Backstitch will later finish the square.

   A clear distinction needs to be made between three-quarter cross stitches and half cross stitches. A three-quarter stitch occupies half of a square diagonally. A half cross stitch is like a normal cross stitch, but only the top diagonal stitch is worked, to give a more delicate effect to the finished design. Stitches worked in this way are indicated quite clearly on the colour keys next to each chart with their own symbols.

BACKSTITCH

Backstitch is used in the projects to give emphasis to a particular foldline, an outline or a shadow. The stitches are worked over the same number of threads as the cross stitch, forming continuous straight or diagonal lines.

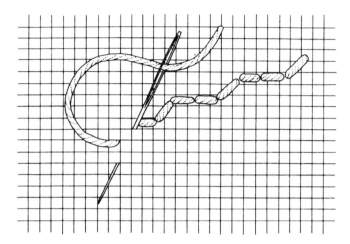

● Make the first stitch from left to right; pass the needle behind the fabric and bring it out one stitch length ahead to the left. Repeat and continue in this way along the line.

FRENCH KNOTS

This stitch is shown on some of the diagrams by a small dot. Where there are several french knots featured in the design, the dots have been omitted from the diagrams to avoid confusion. Where this occurs you should refer to the instructions of the project and the colour photograph.

● To work a french knot, bring your needle and cotton out slightly to the right of where you want your knot to be. Wind the thread once or twice around the needle, depending on how big you want your knot to be, and insert the needle to the left of the point where you brought it out.

Be careful not to pull too hard or the knot will disappear through the fabric. The instructions state the number of strands of cotton to be used for the french knots.

FINISHING

MITRING A CORNER

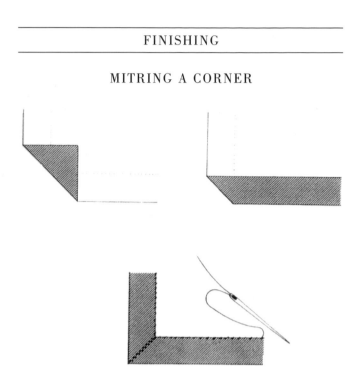

● Press a single hem to the wrong side, the same as the measurement given in the instructions. Open the hem out again and fold the corner of the fabric inwards as shown on the diagram. Refold the hem to the wrong side along the pressed line, and slipstitch in place.

BINDING AN EDGE

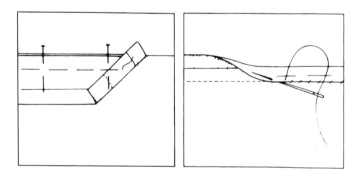

1 Open out the turning on one edge of the bias binding and pin in position on the right side of the fabric, matching the fold to the seamline. Fold over the cut end of the binding. Finish the binding by overlapping the starting point by about 12mm (1/2in). Baste and then machine stitch along the seamline to secure.

2 Fold the binding over the raw edge to the wrong side. Then baste to secure and, using matching sewing thread, neatly hem the binding in place to finish. Finally, press the binding for a neat edge.

PIPED SEAMS

Contrasting piping adds a special decorative finish to a seam, brightening up a plain-coloured fabric, and looks particularly attractive on items such as cushions and cosies. You can also use it to highlight a colour in your embroidery.

You can cover piping cord with either bias-cut fabric of your choice or a bias binding; alternatively, ready-covered piping cord is available in several widths and many colours.

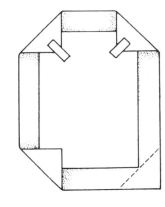

1 To apply piping to your fabric, pin and baste it to the right side of the fabric, with seam lines matching. Clip into the seam allowance where necessary and trim excess fabric.

2 With right sides together, place the second piece of fabric on top, enclosing the piping inside. Baste and then either hand stitch the piping in place or machine stitch, using a zipper foot. Stitch as close to the piping as possible, covering the first line of stitching.

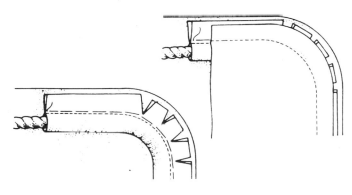

3 To join ends of piping cord together, first overlap the two ends by about 2.5cm (1in). Unpick the two cut ends of bias to reveal the cord. Join the bias strip as shown. Trim and press the seam open. Unravel and splice the two ends of the cord. Fold the bias strip over it, and finish basting around the edge.

MOUNTING EMBROIDERY

The cardboard should be cut to the size of the finished embroidery, with an extra 6mm (¹/₄in) added all round to allow for the recess in the frame.

LIGHTWEIGHT FABRICS

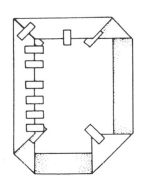

1 Place embroidery face down, with the cardboard centred on top, and basting and pencil lines matching. Begin by folding over the fabric at each corner and securing it with masking tape.

2 Working first on one side and then the other, fold over the fabric on all sides and secure it firmly with pieces of masking tape, placed about 2.5cm (1in) apart. Also neaten the mitred corners with masking tape, pulling the fabric tightly to give a firm, smooth finish.

HEAVIER FABRICS

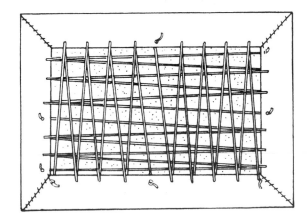

• Lay the embroidery face down, with the cardboard centred on top; fold over the edges of the fabric on opposite sides, making mitred folds at the corners, and lace across, using strong thread. Repeat on the other two sides. Finally, pull up the fabric firmly over the cardboard. Overstitch the mitred corners.

WEDDING CELEBRATIONS

*What better way to
commemorate a wedding or
anniversary than in cross stitch?
In this chapter, there
is a wide range of ideas for
making wedding celebrations
extra special, from place cards
and gift tags to cushions,
table linen and samplers.*

WEDDING ACCESSORIES

YOU WILL NEED

For all the projects:

*Stranded embroidery cotton in the colours
given in the appropriate panel
No24 tapestry needle
Silver thread (DMC code 278, shade 4041)
Fabric glue*

For the Wedding Place Card, with a design area
measuring 10cm × 3.5cm (4in × 1½in):

*6cm × 13cm (2½in × 5in) of white, 18-count
Aida fabric
Card mount, with an aperture measuring
3.5cm × 10cm (1½in × 4in)*

For the Wedding Greetings Card, measuring
15cm × 20cm (6in × 8in) with a cut-out measuring
10cm × 14cm (4in × 5½in):

*12cm × 16cm (4¾in × 6¼in) of white, 26-count
evenweave linen
Purchased greetings card mount, (for
suppliers, see page 256)*

For the Gift Tag, measuring 7.5cm (3in) square with
a cut-out of 5.5cm (2¼in) in diameter:

*7cm (2¾in) square of white, 26-count evenweave
linen
Purchased gift tag (for suppliers, see page 256)*

For the Almond Bag, with a finished size of
9cm × 11.5cm (3½in × 4½in):

*14cm × 16cm (5½in × 6½in) of white, 26-count
evenweave linen
Matching sewing thread
11.5cm × 14cm (4½in × 5½in) of white fabric,
for backing
36cm (14in) of white broderie anglaise,
2.5cm (1in) wide
50cm (20in) of pink ribbon, 6mm (¼in) wide*

•

THE EMBROIDERY

As none of the projects is very large, they may all be
held in the hand when working the embroidery.

Following the correct chart, start the embroidery at
the centre of the design, using two strands of cotton
for all designs except the place card which is worked
with one strand of cotton for the cross stitch. Work
each stitch over either one block or two threads of
fabric in each direction. Make sure that all the top
crosses run in the same direction and that each row
is worked into the same holes as the row before so
that you do not leave a space.

For the silver crosses on the gift tag and almond
bag, use a 100cm (40in) length of silver thread
folded double, but for the silver crosses on the place
card use a 50cm (20in) length of silver thread used
singly. Work the backstitch lines on the almond
bag and place card with one strand of cotton. Blend
one 50cm (20in) length of silver thread with one
50cm (20in) length of light mauve thread for the
stitching on the almond bag and wedding card.

MAKING UP

Gently press the finished embroidery for the cards
and tags on the wrong side and trim to about 12mm
(½in) larger than the cut-out window. Open out the
card and centre your embroidery behind the
aperture, securing with a spot of glue. Fold the card
and secure with another spot of glue.

ALMOND BAG ▼		DMC	ANCHOR	MADEIRA
∕	Light mauve	209	0110	0803
	blended with silver	(+ DMC code 278, shade 4041)		
r	Medium mauve	553	098	0712
o	Light green	470	0266	1502
x	Medium green	937	0268	1504
c	Yellow	3078	0292	0102
s	Silver	Available from DMC only		
		Code 278, shade 4041		

Note: bks lines in medium green.

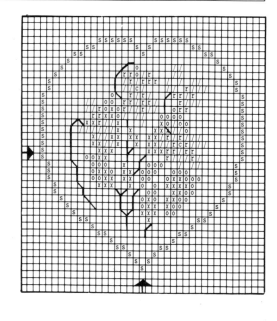

For the almond bag, trim the embroidery to measure 11.5cm × 14cm (4¹⁄₂ in × 5¹⁄₂ in). With right sides together, baste and machine stitch the embroidery to the backing fabric, stitching down the sides and across the bottom, taking a 12mm (¹⁄₂ in) seam allowance.

Turn to the right side. Turn a single 12mm (¹⁄₂ in) hem around the top. Join the short edges of the broderie anglaise with a tiny french seam, then run a gathering thread close to the straight edge of the lace. Pull up the gathers to fit and, with the right side of the lace facing the wrong side of the bag, baste and then machine stitch the broderie anglaise in place around the top. Gently steam press. Fill the bag with almonds and tie it with the ribbon.

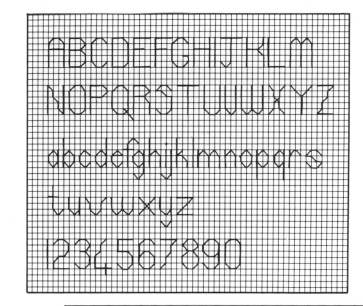

GIFT TAG ▼		DMC	ANCHOR	MADEIRA
X	Medium green	937	0268	1504
C	Yellow	3078	0292	0102
<	Light pink	3689	073	0607
+	Dark pink	3688	066	0605
r	Medium mauve	553	098	0712
S	Silver	Available from DMC only Code 278, shade 4041		

GREETINGS CARD ▼		DMC	ANCHOR	MADEIRA
O	Light green	470	0266	1502
X	Medium green	937	0268	1504
=	Dark green	3345	0269	406
/	Light mauve	209	0110	0803
	blended with silver	(+ DMC code 278, shade 4041)		
r	Medium mauve	553	098	0712
+	Dark mauve	327	0101	0805
C	Yellow	3078	0292	0102

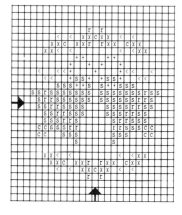

WEDDING PLACE CARD ▼		DMC	ANCHOR	MADEIRA
/	Light mauve	209	0110	0803
r	Medium mauve	553	098	0715
+	Dark mauve	327	0101	0805
C	Yellow	3078	0292	0102
>	White	Blanc	White	White
−	Light grey	762	0397	1804
V	Dark grey	415	0398	1803
S	Silver	Available from DMC only Code 278, shade 4041		
O	Light green	470	0266	1502
X	Medium green	937	0268	1504
=	Dark green	3345	0269	1406

Note: bks the name in medium green.

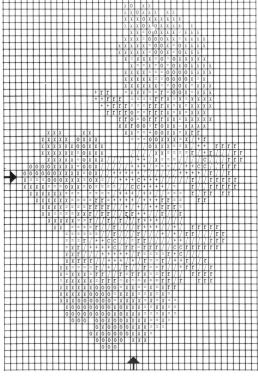

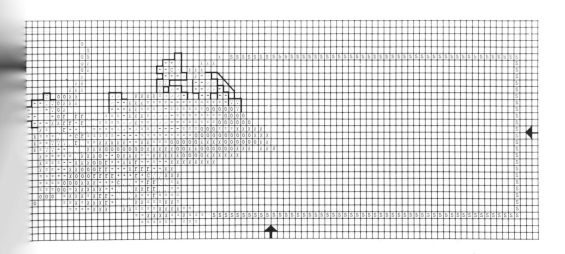

Wedding Ring Cushion

The wedding ring is a tangible
sign of everlasting love and this
beautiful wedding ring cushion,
makes an ideal presentation
for the ring.

WEDDING RING CUSHION

YOU WILL NEED

For the Cushion, measuring 15cm (6in) square:

*25cm (10in) square of cream, 28-count
evenweave fabric
Stranded embroidery cotton in the colours given
in the panel
DMC metallic thread (code 278, shade 4024)
No24 tapestry needle
18cm (7in) square of cream fabric,
for backing
62cm (24in) of gathered lace edging,
2.5cm (1in) wide
Polyester stuffing*

•

THE EMBROIDERY

Prepare the fabric and stretch it in a frame as explained on page 5. Following the chart, start the embroidery at the centre of the design, using two strands of cotton in the needle, or a 100cm (40in) length of gold thread folded double for the cross stitch. Work each stitch over two threads of fabric in each direction, making sure that all the top crosses run in the same direction and that each row is worked into the same holes as the top or bottom of the row before so that you do not leave a space between the rows.

Embroider the single line ring in backstitch using two strands of gold thread, and backstitch the flower outlines with one strand of cotton.

MAKING UP

Gently steam press the finished embroidery on the wrong side and trim to 18cm (7in) square. Join the ends of the lace edging with a narrow french seam and pin and baste it around the edge of the right side of the embroidery. The decorative edge of the lace should face inwards and the straight edge of the lace should be parallel with the edge of the fabric, and just inside the 12mm (½in) seam allowance.

Place the backing fabric over the embroidery, with right sides facing, and baste and stitch through all three layers, stitching through the straight edge of the lace, just within the 12mm (½in) seam allowance, leaving a 7.5cm (3in) gap at one side. Turn the cushion right side out, stuff with the polyester stuffing and slipstitch to close.

WEDDING RING CUSHION ▶		DMC	ANCHOR	MADEIRA
O	Light green	3013	0842	1605
X	Medium green	3052	0861	1509
=	Dark green	3051	0862	1508
C	Cream	712	0926	2101
/	Light beige	3770	933	306
r	Dark beige	3774	881	1909
V	Yellow	745	0300	0111
S	Gold	DMC metallic thread		
		Code 278, shade 4024		

Note: bks the single line ring with two strands of gold, and outline the flowers with dark green.

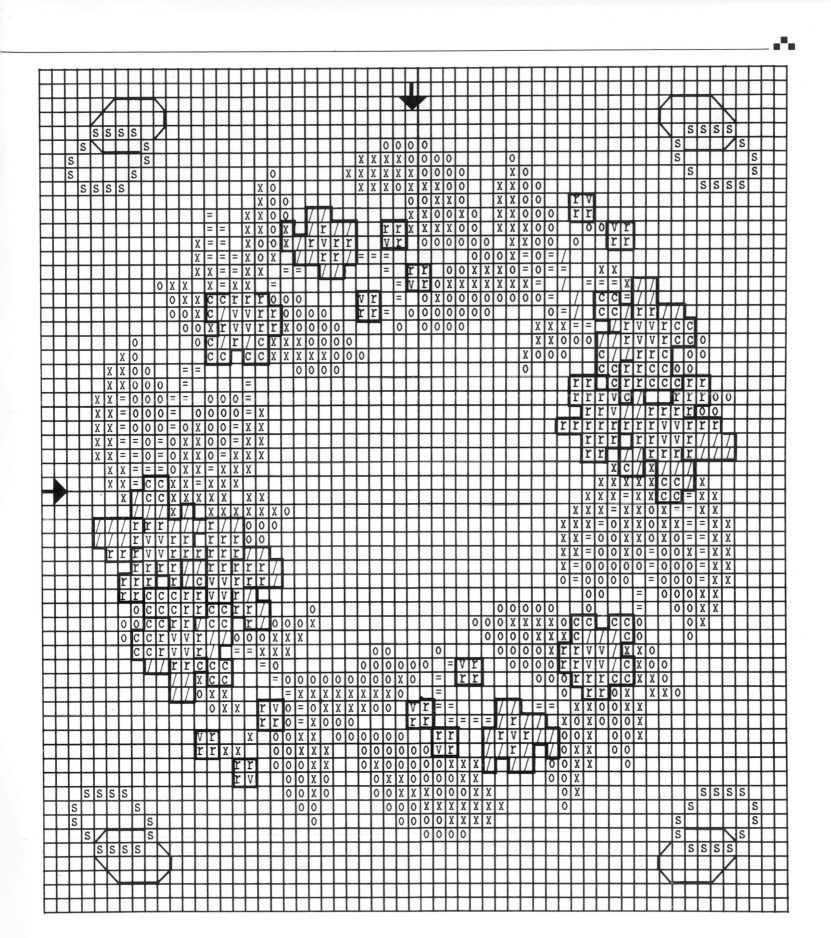

Silver Wedding Bell Pull and Card

This bell pull, with its madonna lily design and silver stitching, and the matching card celebrate 25 years of marriage.

SILVER WEDDING BELL PULL AND CARD

YOU WILL NEED

For the Silver Wedding Card, with a design area measuring 6cm × 10.5cm (2¼in × 4¼in) or 32 stitches by 58 stitches:

16cm × 20cm (6¼in × 8in) of white, 14-count Aida fabric
Stranded embroidery cotton in the colours given in the appropriate panel
No24 tapestry needle
Portrait card mount with an aperture measuring 7cm × 11cm (2¾in × 4½in)
Double-sided tape
Fabric glue

For the Bell Pull, with a design area measuring 36cm × 13cm (14¼in × 5¼in):

45cm (18in) strip of white Aida band, 44 stitches, 8.5cm (3½in) wide
Masking tape
Stranded embroidery cotton in the colours given in the appropriate panel
Silver thread (DMC code 278, shade 4041)
No24 tapestry needle
A pair of bell pull fittings, 10cm (4in) wide (for suppliers, see page 256)
Matching sewing thread

WEDDING CARD

Prepare the fabric and stretch it in a frame as explained on page 5. Following the chart, start the embroidery at the centre of the design using two strands of cotton in the needle for the cross stitch. Work each stitch over one block of fabric in each direction. Make sure that all the top crosses run in the same direction and that each row is worked into the same holes as the row before so that you do not leave a space between the rows. Work the backstitch using one strand of cotton.

Gently press the finished embroidery on the wrong side. Trim to about 12mm (½in) larger than the cut-out aperture. Centre the embroidery behind the aperture and secure with double-sided tape. Fold the backing card inwards and stick with glue for a secure and neat finish.

BELL PULL

Secure each end of the Aida band with masking tape and find the centre by working a vertical and horizontal line of basting stitches. Following the chart, start the embroidery at the centre of the band using two strands of cotton or a 100cm (40in) length of silver thread folded double in the needle for the cross stitch. Work each stitch over one block of fabric in each direction. Make sure that all the top crosses run in the same direction and that each row is worked into the same holes as the row before so that you do not leave a space. Work the backstitch using one strand of cotton.

Gently press the work on the wrong side. Slip the bell pull fittings over each end so that you have

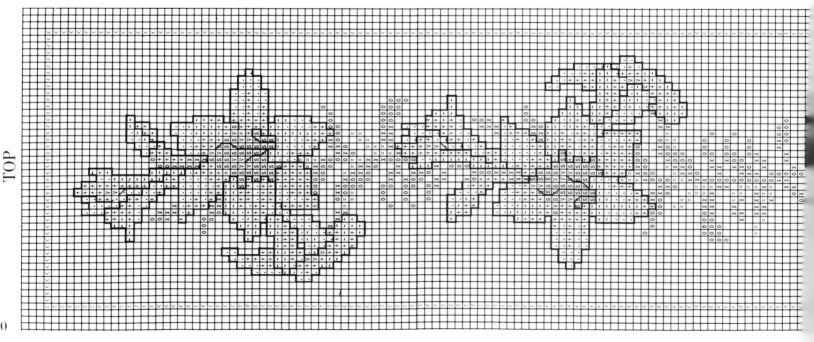

TOP

about 12mm (¹/₂in) between the line of silver stitching and the top and bottom of the bell pull. Turn the raw edge under at the top and bottom and slipstitch in place to the wrong side.

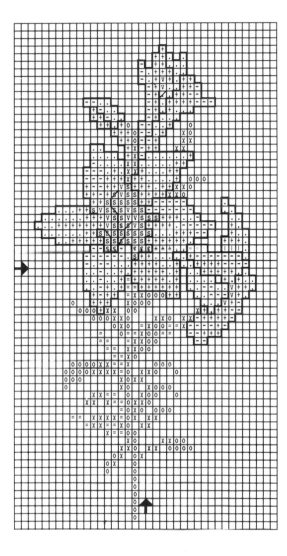

SILVER WEDDING CARD ◄		DMC	ANCHOR	MADEIRA
O	Light green	472	0253	1414
X	Medium green	471	0265	1501
=	Dark green	470	0266	1502
S	Light grey	762	0397	1804
+	Dark grey	415	0398	1803
·	White	Blanc	White	White
−	Cream	746	0926	0101
V	Apricot	948	0933	0306

Note: bks the flower outline in dark green.

BELL PULL ▼		DMC	ANCHOR	MADEIRA
O	Light green	472	0253	1414
X	Medium green	471	0265	1501
=	Dark green	470	0266	1502
S	Light grey	762	0397	1804
+	Dark grey	415	0398	1803
·	White	Blanc	White	White
−	Cream	746	0926	0101
V	Apricot	948	0933	0306
<	Silver	Available from DMC only Code 278, shade 4041		

Note: bks the flower outline in dark green.

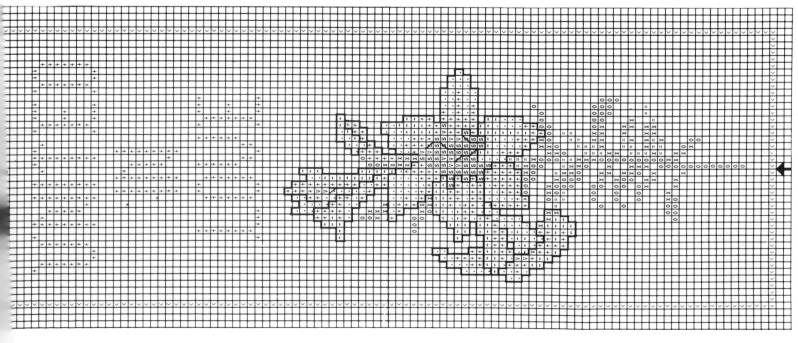

BOTTOM

Silver Wedding Traycloth and Serviette

Afternoon tea will never be the same again with this traycloth and matching serviette embroidered with roses and ribbons.

SILVER WEDDING TRAYCLOTH AND SERVIETTE

For the Traycloth, measuring 33cm × 47cm
(13in × 19in):

*Purchased 26-count traycloth (for suppliers,
see page 256)
Stranded embroidery cotton in the colours given
in the appropriate panel
No24 tapestry needle*

For the Serviette, measuring 40cm (16in) square:

*Purchased 26-count serviette (for suppliers,
see page 256)
Stranded embroidery cotton in the colours given
in the appropriate panel
No24 tapestry needle*

•

PREPARING THE FABRIC

If you prefer not to use ready-prepared table linen,
buy fabric with the same thread count. To prepare
the fabric, mark a line with basting stitches 2.5cm
(1in) from the start of the fringe on the right and left
hand sides and top and bottom of the traycloth. The
point at which the lines intersect in the corners is
where you place your embroidery. For the serviette
measure 2.5cm (1in) in from the right hand and
bottom edges in one corner and mark with basting
stitches. Once again, the point at which the lines
intersect is where you place your embroidery.
Stretch the traycloth or napkin in a frame (see
page 5).

THE EMBROIDERY

Start the embroidery by positioning it following the
mark on the diagram. Using two strands of cotton in
the needle, work each cross stitch over two threads
of fabric in each direction. Make sure that all the top
crosses run in the same direction and that each row
is worked into the same holes as the row before so
that you do not leave a space between the rows.
Work the backstitch with one strand of cotton.
Gently steam press the finished embroidery on the
wrong side to remove all creases.

If you have used evenweave fabric, rather than
ready-prepared table linen, trim to the correct size

(including fringe), and withdraw a thread 12mm
('⁄₂in) in from each edge. Neatly overcast every
alternate thread, and then remove all cross threads
below the stitched line to complete the fringe.

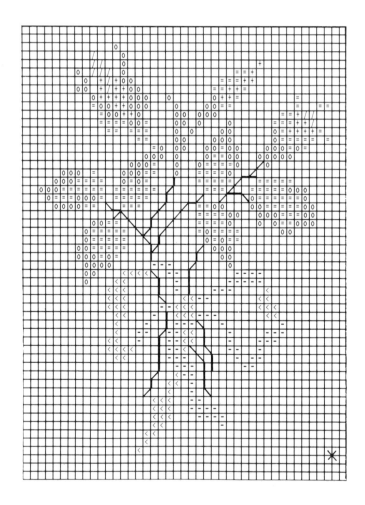

SERVIETTE ▲		DMC	ANCHOR	MADEIRA
⁄	Light peach	353	08	0304
+	Dark peach	352	09	0303
O	Light green	989	0256	1401
=	Dark green	987	0258	1403
–	Light blue	3747	117	901
<	Dark blue	794	0120	0907

Note: bks the flower stems in dark green.

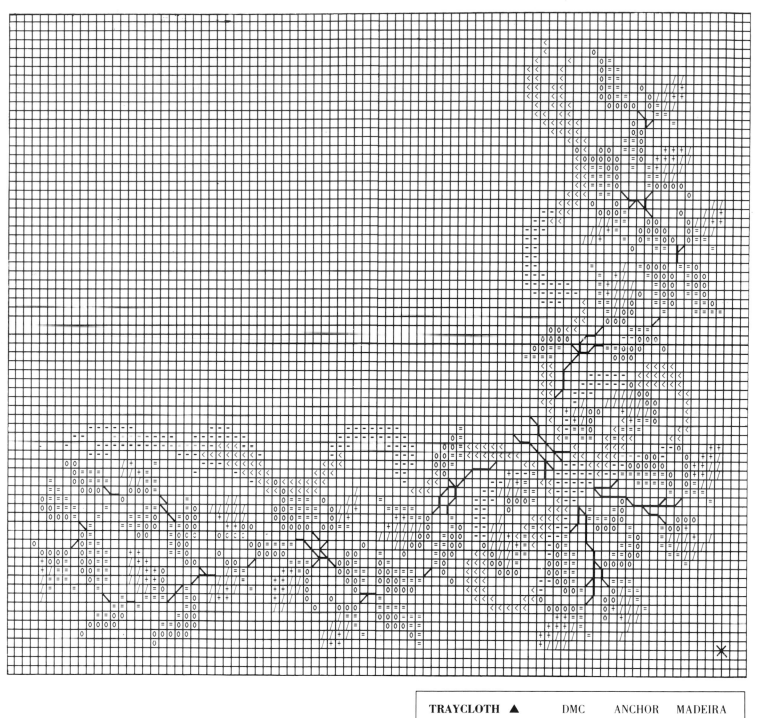

TRAYCLOTH ▲	DMC	ANCHOR	MADEIRA
⟋ Light peach	353	08	0304
+ Dark peach	352	09	0303
⃝ Light green	989	0256	1401
= Dark green	987	0258	1403
− Light blue	3747	117	901
< Dark blue	794	0120	0907

Note: bks the flower stems in dark green.

Ruby Wedding Bowl & Mirror

The vibrant colours of these ruby red roses, as fresh as the day they were cut, decorate a dressing table bowl and handbag mirror.

RUBY WEDDING BOWL & MIRROR

explained in the manufacturer's instructions. Trim
the mirror cover to the size of the paper pattern
provided and, again, mount as explained in the
manufacturer's instructions.

YOU WILL NEED

For the Bowl, with an inset measuring
9cm (3½in) in diameter:

*12cm (4¾in) square of white, 22-count
Hardanger fabric
Stranded embroidery cotton in the colours given
in the appropriate panel
No24 tapestry needle
Glass bowl with prepared lid (for suppliers,
see page 256)*

For the Handbag Mirror, with an inset measuring
6.5cm (2½in):

*10cm (4in) square of white, 18-count
Aida fabric
Stranded embroidery cotton in the colours given
in the appropriate panel
No24 tapestry needle
Handbag mirror with prepared cover (for suppliers,
see page 256)*

●

THE EMBROIDERY

Prepare the fabric and stretch it in a frame as
explained on page 5. Following the appropriate
chart, start the embroidery at the centre of the
design using one strand of cotton in the needle.
Work each stitch over one block of fabric in each
direction. Make sure that all the top crosses run in
the same direction and that each row is worked into
the same holes as the row before so that you do not
leave a space between the rows.

MAKING UP

Gently press the finished embroidery on the wrong
side. Trim the bowl lid to the size of the paper
pattern that is provided with the lid and mount it as

HANDBAG MIRROR ▼		DMC	ANCHOR	MADEIRA
r	Light red	666	046	0210
v	Medium red	304	047	0509
s	Dark red	814	072	0514
x	Medium green	3347	0266	1408
=	Dark green	3345	0268	1406

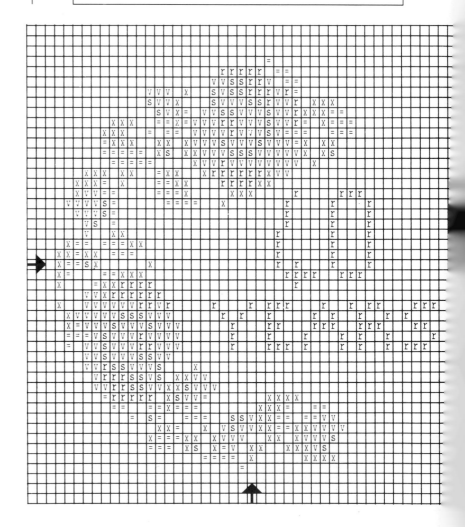

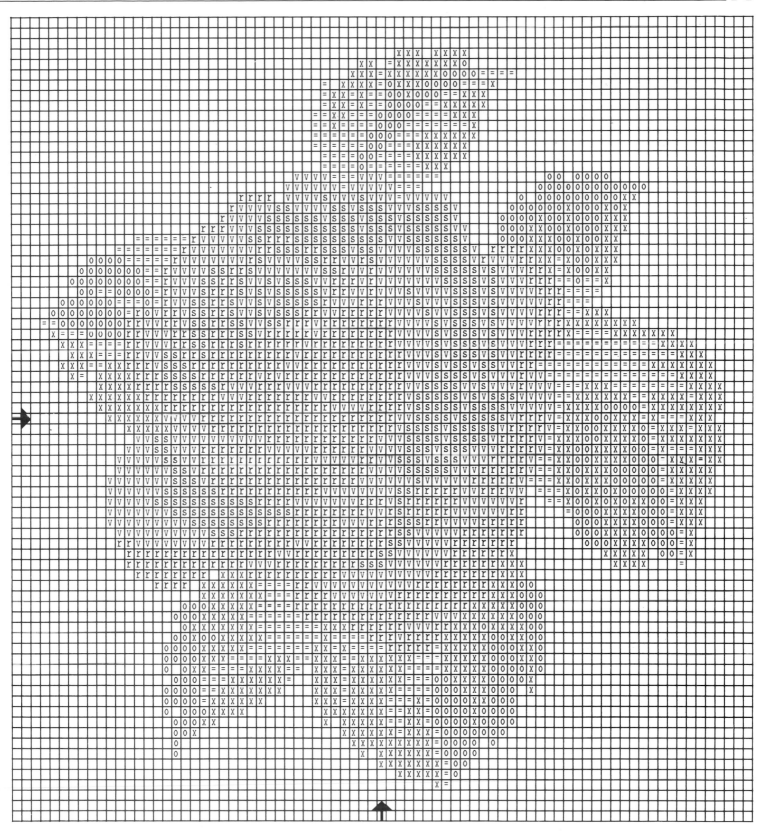

ROSE BOWL ▲		DMC	ANCHOR	MADEIRA
r	Light red	666	046	0210
v	Medium red	304	047	0509
s	Dark red	814	072	0514
o	Light green	3348	0265	1409
x	Medium green	3347	0266	1408
=	Dark green	3345	0268	1406

Golden Wedding Photograph Album

Delicate cream daisies decorate
this photograph album which
you can use to hold your record
in pictures of fifty happy years
of marriage.

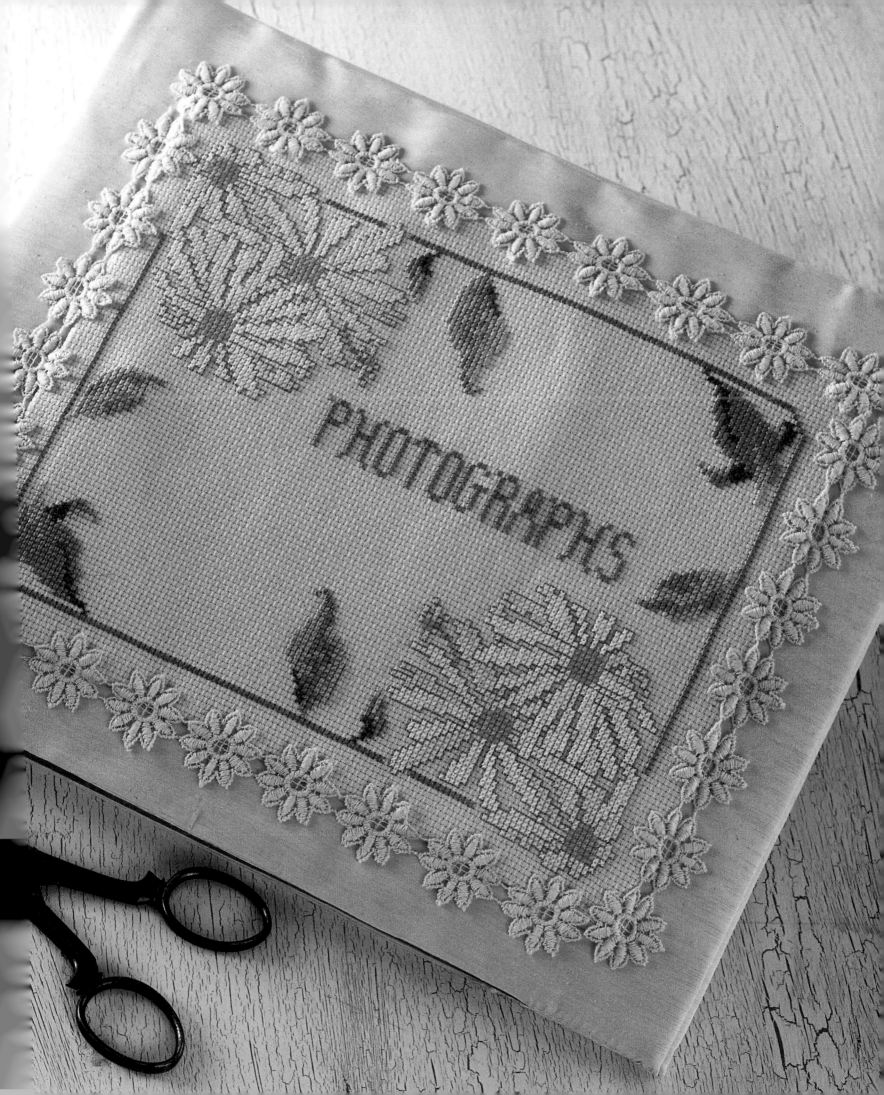

GOLDEN WEDDING PHOTOGRAPH ALBUM

YOU WILL NEED

*33cm × 28cm (13in × 11in) of cream, 14-count
Aida fabric
Stranded embroidery cotton in the colours given
in the panel
No24 tapestry needle
Photograph album of your choice
Cream satin-type fabric, to cover photograph album
Cream backing fabric, the same size as the
cream satin
1m (40in) of cream lace daisies
Fabric glue*

•

THE EMBROIDERY

Prepare the Aida fabric and stretch it in a frame as explained on page 5. Following the chart, start the embroidery at the centre of the design, using two strands of cotton in the needle for the cross stitch. Work each stitch over a block of fabric in each direction, making sure that all the top crosses run in the same direction and that each row is worked into the same holes as the top or bottom of the row before, so that you do not leave a space between the rows. Work the backstitch using one strand of cotton in the needle.

MAKING UP

Calculate the amount of satin fabric you require by measuring your album from front cover edge to back cover edge when it is closed, adding an extra 15cm (6in), then measuring from the top edge to the bottom edge, adding an extra 2.5cm (1in). Cut out a piece of cream satin-type fabric, and cream backing fabric, following these measurements. With right sides together, baste and sew the backing fabric and satin-type fabric together, 12mm (½in) from the edge on the two long sides and one of the short sides. Turn to the right side, press gently and slipstitch the opening along the edge. Wrap the cover around the closed album and turn under the same amount to the inside of the album at the front and back to make the flap. Slipstitch at the top and bottom to make a removable jacket.

Gently steam press the embroidered fabric on the wrong side. Trim to 30cm × 23cm (12in × 9in), then turn under 12mm (½in) on all sides, mitring the

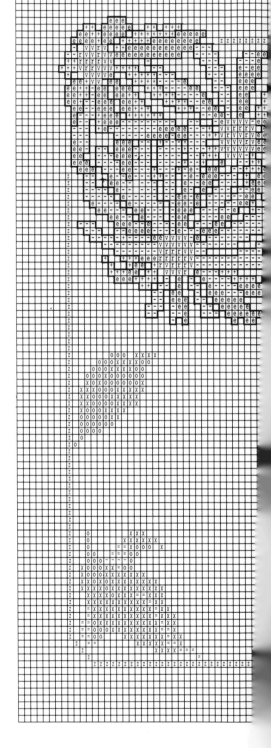

corners as explained on page 8. Position the embroidered panel centrally on the front of the cover and pin in place. Remove the cover from the album and baste and slipstitch the embroidered panel in place. Glue the lace daisies in place around the edge of the embroidered fabric. Replace the cover on the album.

PHOTOGRAPH ALBUM	▲	DMC	ANCHOR	MADEIRA
o Light green		3348	0265	1409
x Medium green		3347	0266	1408
= Dark green		3345	0268	1406
+ Light yellow		3078	0292	0102
r Dark yellow		743	0305	0133
e Cream		746	0926	0101
− White		Blanc	White	White
v Orange		742	0303	0144
z Beige		642	0392	1906

Note: bks the flower outlines in beige.

Diamond Wedding Sampler

The soft cream and pink roses on this sampler are a gentle reminder of sixty happy years spent together.

DIAMOND WEDDING
SAMPLER

YOU WILL NEED

For the Diamond Wedding Sampler, with a design area measuring 18cm × 22.5cm (7in × 9in), or 123 stitches by 99 stitches, here in a frame measuring 23cm × 28cm (9¼in × 11in):

28cm × 33cm (11in × 13in) of cream, 14-count Aida fabric
Stranded embroidery cotton in the colours given in the panel
No24 tapestry needle
Strong thread, for lacing across the back
Cardboard, for mounting
Frame of your choice

●

THE EMBROIDERY

Prepare the fabric and stretch it in a frame as explained on page 5. Following the chart, start the embroidery at the centre of the design using two strands of cotton in the needle. Work each cross stitch over one block of fabric in each direction. Make sure that all the top crosses run in the same direction and that each row is worked into the same holes as the row before so that you do not leave a space between the rows. Add the appropriate date in dark beige and year in light beige, using the chart shown opposite for the alphabet and numbers.

MAKING UP

Gently steam press the finished embroidery on the wrong side and mount it as explained on page 9. Choose a mount and frame to complement your embroidery colour and complete following the instructions on page 9.

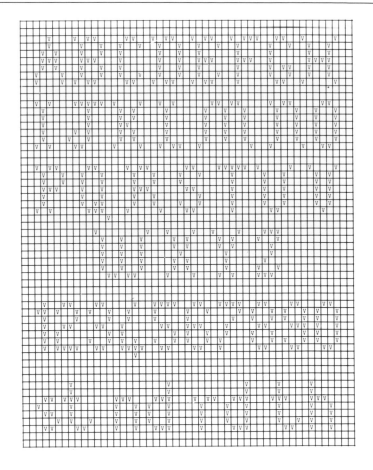

DIAMOND WEDDING SAMPLER ▶		DMC	ANCHOR	MADEIRA
s	Light green	3052	0861	509
/	Medium green	3363	262	602
x	Dark green	3362	263	601
n	Light pink	776	025	0503
=	Dark pink	899	027	0505
e	Cream	746	0926	0101
<	Light beige	642	0392	1906
+	Dark beige	640	0393	1905
r	Blue	800	0128	0908
o	Yellow	3078	0292	0102

THE NEW ARRIVAL

The arrival of a new baby
always provides a marvellous
excuse to start stitching, and
in this chapter are featured
some delightful cross stitch baby
gifts, ranging from clown towels
and a hen cot cover to
a matching bib, mug
and placemat.

BABY'S GIFT SET

YOU WILL NEED

For the *Three Little Pigs* towel, measuring
46cm × 29cm (18in × 11½in), with a design area
measuring 25.5cm × 4cm (10in × 1½in) or
for the bibs, each measuring approximately
18.5 × 15cm (7¼in × 6in), with a design area
measuring 6.5cm × 5cm (2½in × 2in), *Duck*,
5cm × 4.5cm (2in × 1¾in), and *Donkey*:

*Stranded embroidery cotton in the colours given
in the appropriate panel
No24 tapestry needle
Chosen item (for suppliers, see page 256)
Strong thread to match the Aida band (towel only)*

*NOTE: the towel already has the lace-edged Aida
band attached to it; if you wish to add embroidery
to an ordinary towel, you can purchase Aida band
from specialist suppliers (see page 256) and attach it
to the towel once you have decorated it with your
chosen motif.*

•

THE EMBROIDERY

There is no need to use a hoop or frame for these
small items. For the bibs, decide where you intend to
position your motif and start stitching from
the centre outwards, using two strands of thread
in the needle for cross stitching and one for
backstitching.

The Aida band on the towel is attached on three
sides, leaving one long edge free so that you can
hold the band apart from the towel when cross
stitching. Mark the horizontal and vertical centre
lines of the towel with lines of basting stitches in a
light-coloured thread, and stitch from the centre,
again using two strands of thread in the needle for
cross stitches and one strand for backstitching.
Leave six Aida blocks between pigs.

FINISHING THE TOWEL

When you have finished embroidering the Aida
band, slipstitch the lower edge of the Aida band to
the towel, using matching thread and stitching along
the join between the Aida band and the lave trim.

THREE LITTLE PIGS ▼		ANCHOR	DMC	MADEIRA
■	Dark pink	895	223	0812
+	Blue	146	799	0911
▪	Pink	894	224	0813
✕	Grey	8581	646	1812
	Dark grey*	400	317	1714

Note: bks around pigs in dark grey (*used for backstitching only).*

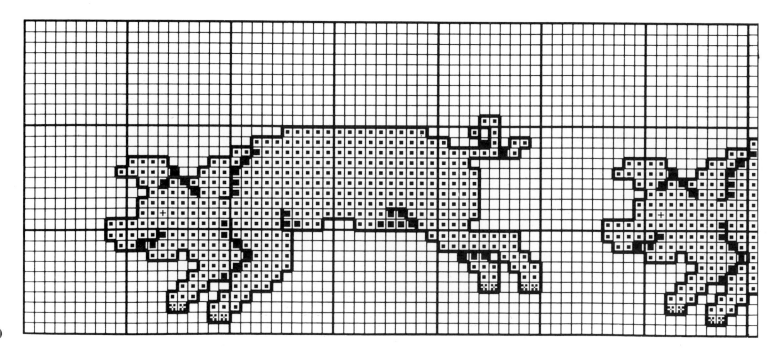

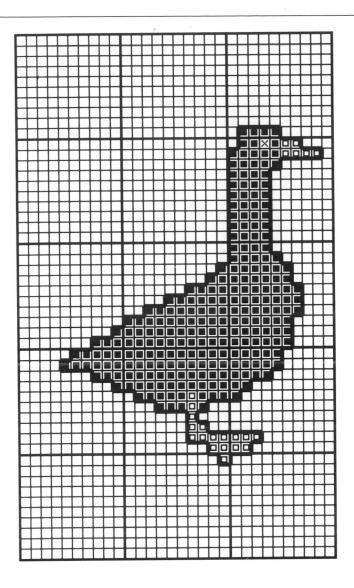

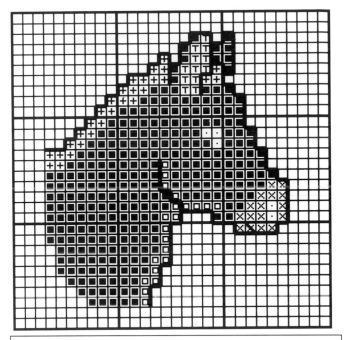

Note: bks around the duck in blue, using one strand of thread in the needle.

DONKEY ▲	ANCHOR	DMC	MADEIRA
+ Rich brown	358	433	2008
T Pink	893	225	0814
⊠ Stone	392	642	1906
■ Pinkish brown	378	841	1911
☐ Darker pinkish brown	379	840	1912
· Black	403	310	Black

Note: bks around the donkey in rich brown, using one strand of thread in the needle.

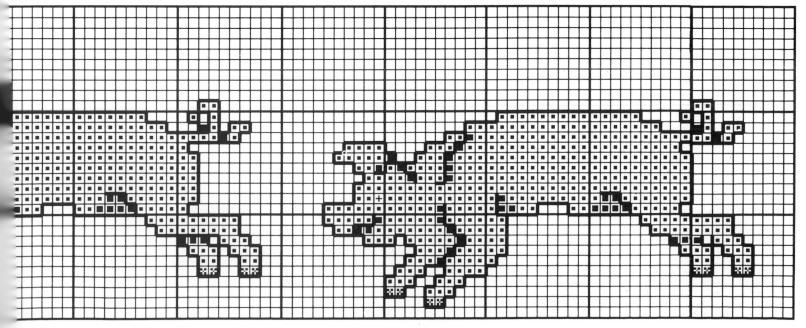

Bib, Mug and Placemat

The naughty puppy who decorates these delightful items will bring a smile to any child's face. These three projects would make ideal presents for a new member of the family.

BIB, MUG AND PLACEMAT

YOU WILL NEED

For the Bib, with a design area of 5cm × 7.5cm (2in × 3in), or 27 stitches by 42 stitches:

Purchased bib (for suppliers, see page 256)
Stranded embroidery cotton in the colours given
in the appropriate panel
No24 tapestry needle

For the Mug, with a single design area of 6.5cm × 5cm (2½in × 2in), or 34 stitches by 27 stitches:

Purchased Stitch-a-Mug (for suppliers, see page 256)
Stranded embroidery cotton in the colours given in
the appropriate panel
No24 tapestry needle

For the Placemat, measuring 42.5cm × 29cm (17in × 11½in), with a design area of 22cm × 5cm (8½in × 2in), or 120 stitches by 29 stitches:

44cm × 30cm (17½in × 12in) of sky blue, 14-count
Aida fabric
Stranded embroidery cotton in the colours given
in the appropriate panel
No24 tapestry needle
2m (2¼yd) of blue bias binding, 2.5cm (1in) wide
Matching sewing thread

•

THE BIB AND MUG

For the bib, mark the central horizontal and vertical design lines with basting stitches and stretch the bib in a frame, following the instructions on page 5. Start the embroidery at the centre of the design, using three strands of thread in the needle for the cross stitch, and two strands of thread for the backstitch.

For the mug, the vinyl strip measuring 25cm × 9cm (10in × 3½in) should meet where the handle is attached. You can centre the design on the vinyl strip and stitch it once, or stitch the design twice so that it can be seen on each side of the mug. If you stitch the design twice, measure 7cm (2¾in) from each end of the strip and baste vertically, to give the vertical centre design lines. Start the embroidery in the centre of the design, using two strands of

thread in the needle. When complete, slip the strip back into the mug and snap the inner shell back into place.

THE PLACEMAT

Prepare the edges of the fabric and mark the central vertical design line of the fabric with basting stitches. Measure 9cm (3½in) up from the bottom (long edge) of the fabric and baste for the central horizontal design line. Stretch the fabric in a frame, following the instructions on page 5. Start the embroidery at the centre of the design, using two strands of thread in the needle for the cross stitch and one strand for the backstitch. Gently steam press the finished embroidery on the wrong side.

To round off the corners of the fabric, place a cup against each corner and lightly mark the fabric with a pencil. Trim off the excess corner fabric. Pin, baste, and machine stitch the bias binding to the wrong side of the fabric, matching raw edges. Fold the bias binding to the right side and carefully topstitch in position. Press the completed placemat.

PLACEMAT ▼		DMC	ANCHOR	MADEIRA
◤	Dark brown	434	310	2009
⊖	Medium brown	436	363	2011
Ⴖ	Honey	739	368	2014
╱	White	White	2	White
■	Black	310	403	Black
▬	Green	368	214	1310
+	Light green	369	213	1309

Note: bks outlines in medium brown.

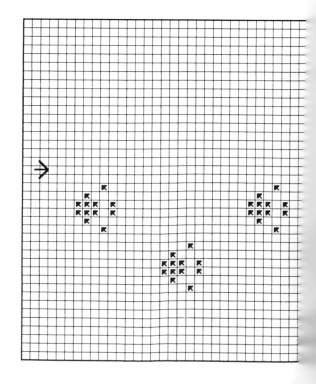

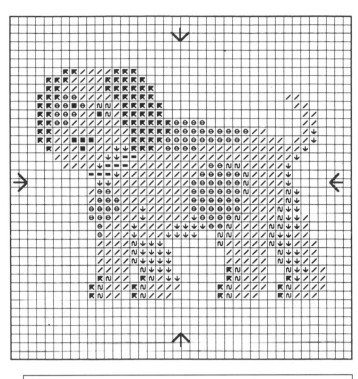

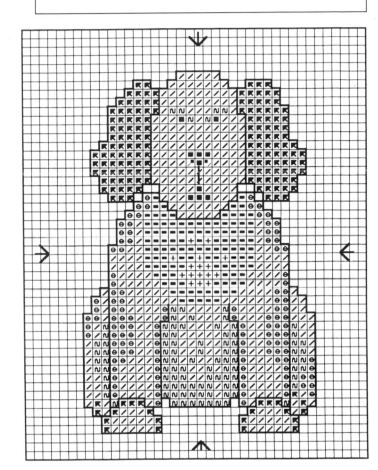

BIB ▼		DMC	ANCHOR	MADEIRA
⬈	Dark brown	434	310	2009
⊖	Medium brown	436	363	2011
∾	Honey	739	368	2014
╱	White	White	2	White
■	Black	310	403	Black
▬	Green	368	214	1310
+	Light green	369	213	1309

Note: bks outlines in medium brown.

MUG ▲		DMC	ANCHOR	MADEIRA
⬈	Dark brown	434	310	2009
⊖	Medium brown	436	363	2011
∾	Light brown	437	362	2012
↓	Honey	738	361	2013
╱	Light honey	739	368	2014
■	Black	310	403	Black
▬	Green	368	214	1310

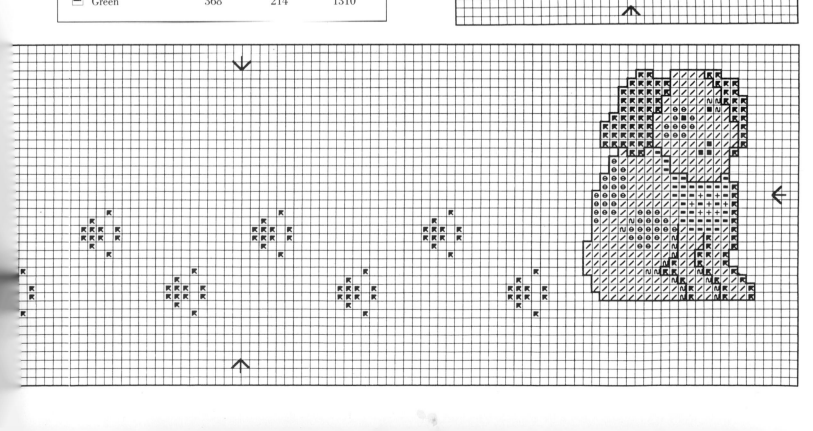

Alphabet Picture

Learning can be fun - teach your children their alphabet and numbers with the help of this colourful clown, juggling with letters. The bright colours make the picture an attractive addition to a nursery or a child's bedroom.

ALPHABET PICTURE

YOU WILL NEED

For the Picture, measuring 48.5cm × 41cm (19in × 16in) unframed:

56.5cm × 49cm (22in × 19in) of white, 14-count Aida fabric
Stranded embroidery cotton in the colours given in the panel
No24 tapestry needle
48.5cm × 41cm (19in × 16in) of mounting board
Picture frame of your choice

NOTE: *The embroidery can either be set directly in a frame or within a mount. A double mount was used here, to create a two-tone border around the picture.*

•

THE EMBROIDERY

Prepare the fabric, marking the horizontal and vertical centre lines with basting stitches in a light-coloured thread, and stretch it in a frame (see page 5). Following the chart, start the embroidery at the centre of the design, using two strands of thread in the needle. Finish with the backstitching, using one strand of thread in the needle.

Leaving the basting stitches in position, gently steam press the finished embroidery on the wrong side.

MOUNTING

You can use either of the methods described on page 9 to mount your finished embroidery, using the basted centre lines as guidelines to ensure that you centre the embroidery over the mounting board. To achieve a smooth finish, you may find that it is helpful to secure the fabric to one edge of the board with pins, working from the centre point out to both corners, and then repeat for the opposite side, to make sure that the fabric is even and taut. Secure with tape or lacing, and then repeat for the remaining sides. Carefully remove basting stitches from the mounted embroidery.

If you are setting the mounted fabric in the frame yourself, use rustproof pins to secure the backing board, and seal the back of the picture with broad tape, to ensure that dust cannot enter the frame.

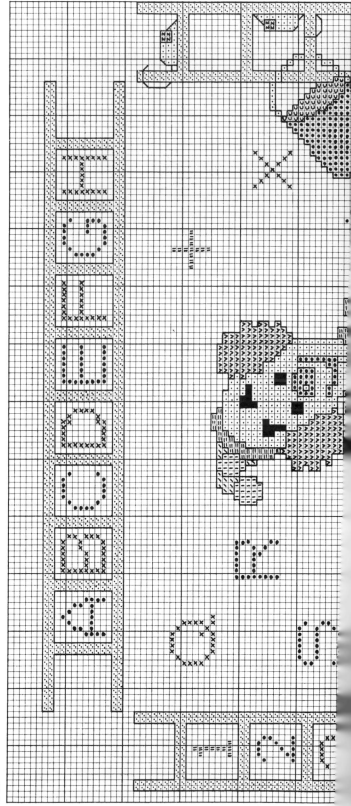

TOP

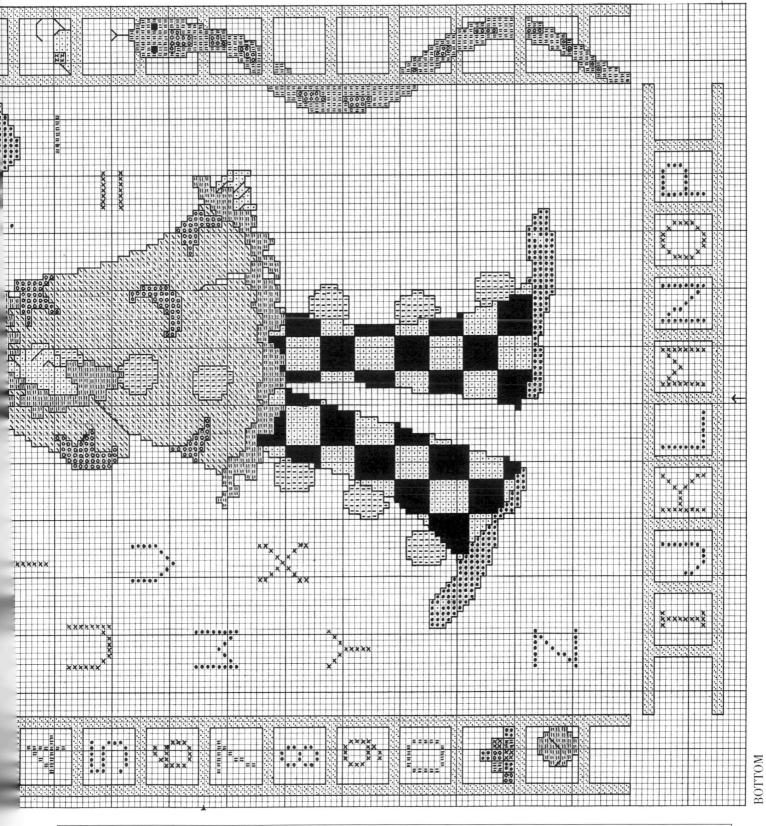

BOTTOM

THE JUGGLER ▲		DMC	ANCHOR	MADEIRA			DMC	ANCHOR	MADEIRA
●	Bright Christmas red	666	46	0210	∴	Tan brown	436	363	2011
X	Royal blue	797	132	0912	·	White	White	2	White
‖	Dark emerald green	910	228	1301	Z	Peach	353	8	0304
■	Black	310	403	Black	╱	Dark lilac	333	119	0903
=	Medium cranberry	602	63	0702	V	Pumpkin orange	971	316	0203
⌷	Bright chartreuse green	704	256	1308	C	Garnet red	816	20	0512
○	Dark lemon yellow	444	291	0108					

Note: bks with black.

49

Butterfly Motifs

Cross-stitched butterflies in delicate blues and greens make a charming addition to baby clothes, whether for a little boy or a girl. Using the waste canvas technique, these small motifs can be stitched to a wide range of purchased garments.

BUTTERFLY MOTIFS

YOU WILL NEED

For each Motif:

*14-count waste canvas (for suppliers, see page 256) –
a piece approximately 2.5cm (1in) larger all
around than the finished motif(s)
Stranded embroidery cotton in the colours
given in panel
Sharp-pointed needle
Tweezers*

*NOTE: for best results, use garments made of non-
stretch fabrics. If you are not stitching all the designs,
you may not require all the colours listed in the key –
check your chosen chart to see which symbols are
used and which threads you will need.*

●

THE EMBROIDERY

Centre the waste canvas over the area where the motif is to be stitched and pin it in position; use the blue threads in the canvas to ensure that the finished embroidery lies straight on the garment, aligning them either with the weave of the fabric or with the seams of the garment, whichever is appropriate. Start the design from the centre, treating each pair of canvas threads as one. The pins may be removed after a few stitches have secured the canvas to the garment.

Following the chart, cross stitch in the usual manner, using two strands of thread in the sharp-pointed needle; take care to stitch through the holes and not the canvas, as the latter would make it difficult to withdraw the threads. Finish with the backstitching, again using two strands of thread.

●

FINISHING

When you have finished the embroidery, cut away surplus canvas, leaving about 12mm (½in) of waste canvas around the design. Either dampen the right side with slightly warm water and leave it for a few minutes until the sizing in the canvas softens, or hand wash in lukewarm water with a mild soap, rinse in cool water, then roll the garment in a towel to absorb excess water (do not wring it, as this may twist the threads). Gently remove the canvas threads, one at a time, with tweezers. The threads should

come out easily, but the operation requires patience; if you try to remove several threads at once this could spoil your embroidery. Dry and press the garment according to the manufacturer's instructions.

FURTHER IDEAS

These little motifs can be used in many ways. You might, for example, place them one beneath the other down the front of a dressing gown, or use a range of sizes on the same outfit. If you choose, you can easily change the colours to match a particular garment, as long as you have three tones each of two different colours.

As already pointed out, it is not easy to use the waste canvas technique with stretch fabrics; one way to overcome the problem is to iron a small piece of interfacing to the back of the area where you want to stitch your motif, then use waste canvas in the normal way.

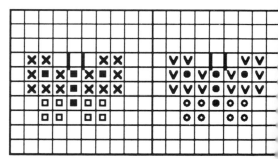

BABYSUIT

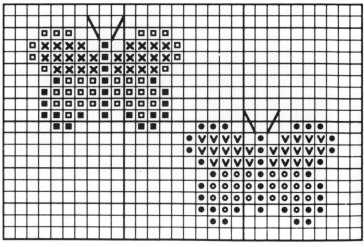

BABYGRO

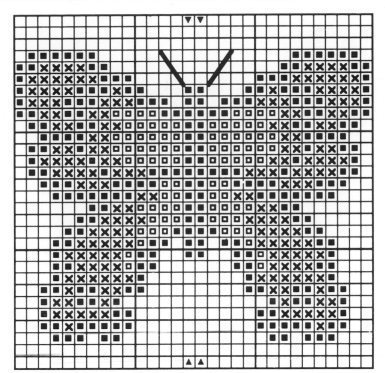

BLUE TOWEL

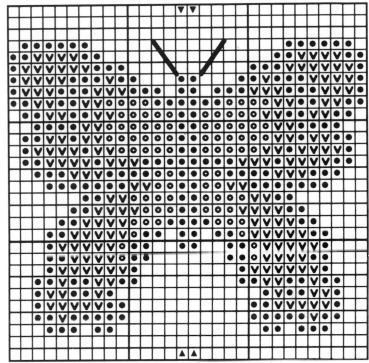

GREEN TOWEL

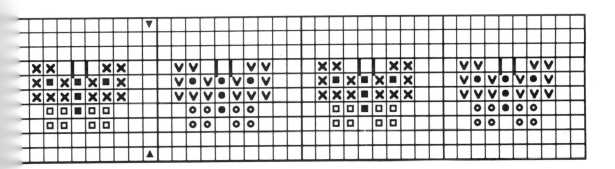

BABYSUIT (SLEEVE)

BUTTERFLY MOTIFS		ANCHOR	DMC	MADEIRA
■	Medium blue	146	798	1012
□	Light blue	145	799	1013
☒	Pale blue	144	800	1014
●	Medium green	205	912	1213
○	Light green	204	913	1212
☑	Pale green	203	563	1211

Note: make the antennae with straight stitches, using medium blue for blue butterflies and medium green for the green ones.

Clown
Towels

Children of any age would be
delighted to receive one of these
'tumbling clown' towels as a gift.
The blues, purples, pinks and
yellows used in the designs make
them suitable for towels in a wide
range of colours.

CLOWN TOWELS

YOU WILL NEED

For each embroidered Towel:

*A strip of white, 14-count Aida band,
10cm (4in) deep and 2.5cm (1in) longer than the
width of your towel
Stranded embroidery cotton in the colours given in
the panel
No24 tapestry needle
White sewing thread
Towel of your choice*

*NOTE: You can, as here, stitch Aida band to any
suitable towel. Alternatively, you can purchase
towels that have an Aida band either inset into the
towel or already attached, along one long edge only
(for suppliers, see page 256).*

Mark the centre of the Aida band both ways with
lines of basting stitches. Before you begin to
stitch, work out how many repeats/clowns will fit
comfortably across the width of your chosen towel.
To achieve a balanced effect, calculate this by
working from the centre outwards, bearing in mind
that you must leave a 12mm ($\frac{1}{2}$in) seam allowance
at each short end. You can easily change the number of empty Aida blocks between clowns, if necessary. There is ample thread for several repeats of
these designs; for variety, you might choose to
change around the colours of the outfits on repeated motifs.

Starting from the centre and working outwards,
stitch the cross stitch design on the Aida band, using
two strands of thread in the needle and making sure
that the top stitches lie in the same direction
throughout. Finish with the backstitching, this time
using one strand of thread in the needle. Gently
steam press the embroidery from the wrong side and
remove basting stitches.

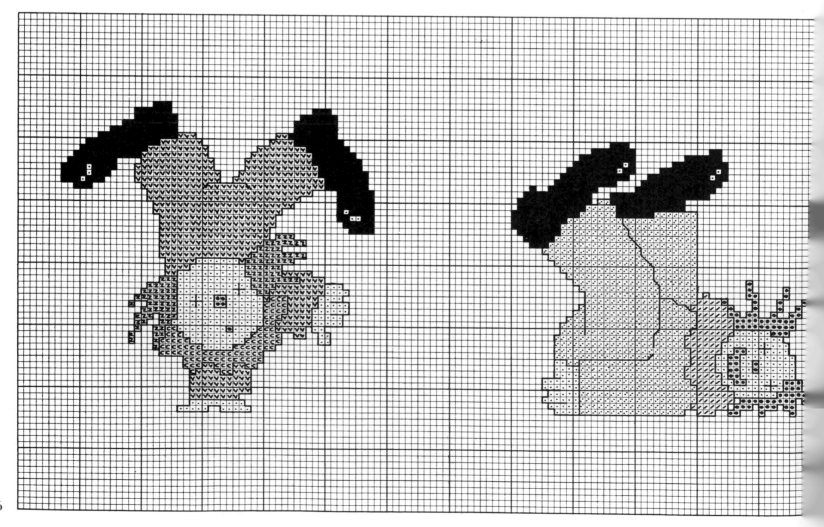

MAKING UP

Turn under a 12mm (½in) hem at each short end, and baste the Aida band to the towel in the desired position. When you are happy with the result, machine stitch the band to the towel.

TUMBLING CLOWNS ▼		DMC	ANCHOR	MADEIRA
Z	Chartreuse green	703	238	1307
●	Bright Christmas red	666	46	0210
·	White	White	2	White
X	Aqua	959	186	1113
C	Periwinkle blue	340	118	0902
L	Cranberry	603	62	0701
╱	Fuchsia purple	3608	86	0709
V	Medium yellow	744	301	0112
■	Royal blue	797	132	0912
II	Very light cranberry	605	50	0613
=	Nile green	954	204	1211
▼	Light pumpkin orange	970	316	0204
··	Delft blue	809	130	0909
	Medium steel grey*	317	400	1714

Note: bks with medium steel grey (*used for bks only).*

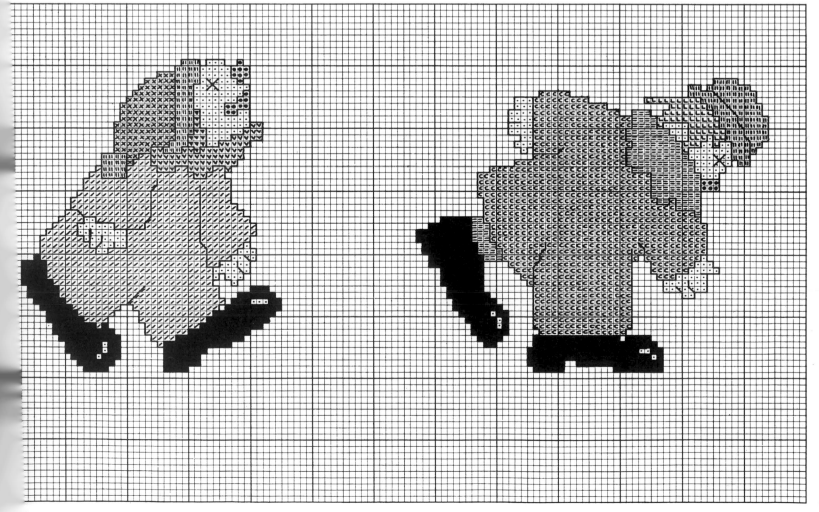

Hen Cot Cover

The snuggly soft fabric of this cot cover/shawl, which is decorated with a simple repeated pattern of bright brown hens, will keep baby warm and cosy. The hen motifs could also be used for pretty birthday cards.

HEN COT COVER

To make the Cot Cover, measuring
90cm × 75.5cm (35$\frac{1}{2}$in × 29$\frac{3}{4}$in) excluding
the fringe:

109cm × 94cm (43in × 37in) of Anne cloth
Stranded embroidery cotton in the colours given
in the panel
No24 tapestry needle
Matching sewing thread

NOTE: Anne cloth is a specially-produced evenweave fabric, divided by bands of contrast weaving into squares, suitable for cross-stitched motifs; for suppliers see page 256.

•

THE EMBROIDERY

Refer to the diagram and position the motifs as follows:

1 Hen facing to the right,
2 Sitting hen, facing right,
3 Sitting hen, facing left.

Mark the centre of each square that is to contain a hen motif with horizontal and vertical lines of basting stitches in a light-coloured thread. For each motif, set the fabric in a hoop (see page 5) and count out from the centre to start stitching at a point convenient to you. To avoid marking the fabric, take the fabric from the hoop at the end of each embroidery session.

Complete the cross stitching, using three strands of thread in the needle and making sure that all top stitches run in the same direction. Finish the standing hens by backstitching around the legs and claws, using one strand of dark brown in the needle.

Remove the embroidery from the hoop. Gently handwash the finished piece, if necessary, and lightly press with a steam iron on the wrong side.

FINISHING

Using matching sewing thread and a machine zigzag stitch, sew along the outer of the two bold white lines of Anne cloth, around the outside of the blank squares, enclosing an area approximately 90cm × 75.5cm (35$\frac{1}{2}$in × 29$\frac{3}{4}$in). Trim the cover to leave an allowance of 4cm (1$\frac{1}{2}$in) beyond the zigzag stitching. On each side, carefully remove parallel threads back to the stitched line, and smooth out the resulting fringe.

		1		
	2		3	
		1		
	2		3	

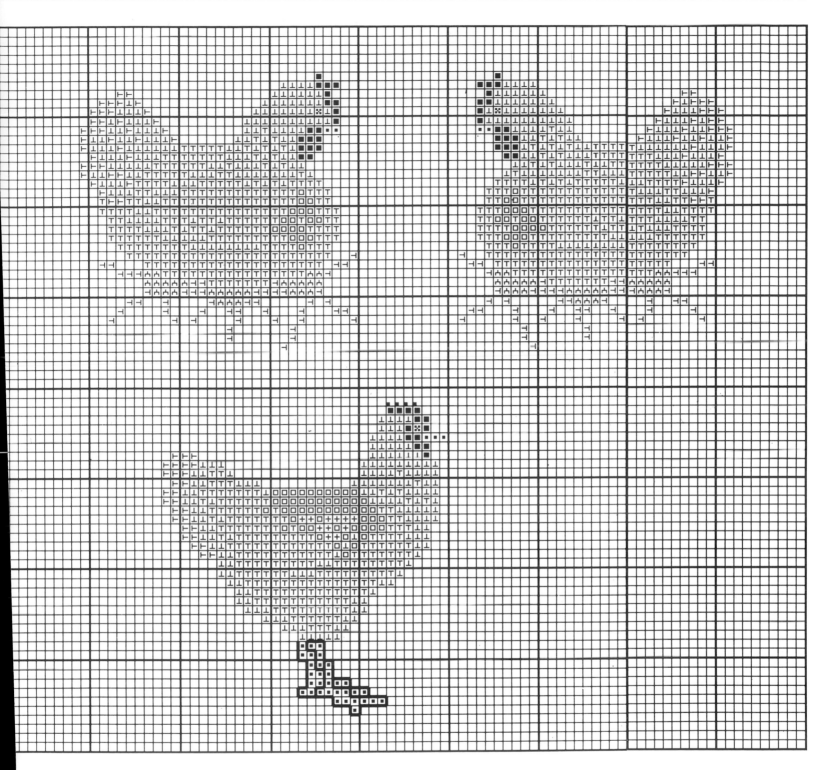

HENS ▲		ANCHOR	DMC	MADEIRA
■	Red	19	347	0407
+	Light rust	369	3776	2302
T	Brown	370	400	2305
⊢	Dark brown	380	801	2007
⌐	Golden brown	1045	436	2011
▪	Straw	887	734	1610
✕	Black	403	310	Black
☐	Rust	349	301	2306
⊥	Rich brown	357	300	2304
⊣	Pale gold	361	676	2208

Note: bks legs and claws in dark brown.

Story Book Picture

Straight from the pages of a story book come Cinderella and her Ugly Sisters, Snow White and the seven dwarfs, Sleeping Beauty and the Pied Piper – a band of friends guaranteed to dance in and out of the dreams of any child.

STORY BOOK PICTURE

For the Picture, set in a frame with an aperture measuring 29cm × 24cm (11½in × 9½in):

40cm × 35cm (16in × 14in) of cream, 11-count Aida fabric
Stranded embroidery cotton in the colours given in the panel
No24 tapestry needle
A frame with an aperture as specified above
Firm card to fit the frame
Lightweight synthetic batting/wadding, the same size as the card
Strong thread and cardboard, for mounting
Glue stick

●

THE EMBROIDERY

Prepare the fabric (see page 5), and mark horizontal and vertical centre lines with basting stitches in a light-coloured thread. Mount the fabric in a frame (see page 5) and start the design from the centre.

Following the chart, complete all the cross stitching first, using two strands of thread in the needle. These designs contain three-quarter stitches (see page 7), which are shown on the chart by the smaller symbols, and should be stitched in the corners indicated. Be careful not to take dark threads across the back of the work in such a way that they show through on the right side. Backstitch the outline, using one strand of navy blue thread. Finally, stitch the stars with one strand of navy blue thread in the needle; stitch one long single line for each of the sides of the stars.

FINISHING

Remove the embroidery from the frame and wash if necessary, then press lightly on the wrong side, using a steam iron. Spread glue evenly on one side of the mounting card, and lightly press the batting (wadding) to the surface. Lace the embroidery over the padded surface (see page 9), using the basting stitches (if any) to check that the embroidery is centred over the card.

Remove basting stitches; place the mounted embroidery in the frame, and assemble the frame according to the manufacturer's instructions.

STORY BOOK PICTURE		ANCHOR	DMC	MADEIRA			ANCHOR	DMC	MADEIRA
−	White	1	White	White	◇	Pale lilac	108	210	0802
╱	Pale yellow	301	744	0110	◆	Medium lilac	111	208	0804
↑	Yellow beige	307	783	2212	−	Brown	371	433	2303
·	Pale peach	8	353	0304	☐	Pinky red	39	309	0507
⸬	Medium peach	9	352	0303		Navy blue*	127	939	1009
V	Apple green	241	703	1401					
▲	Medium green	210	367	1312					
○	Powder blue	144	800	1002					
●	Medium blue	145	799	1004					

Note: bks outline and stars in navy blue* (*used for backstitching only), using one strand of thread in the needle.

Baby's Coverlet

Could any child - or mother - resist these bright, jolly clowns? This wonderfully soft and practical Afghan fabric, featuring 13cm (5in) squares suitable for small cross stitch motifs, is easily washable, making it ideal for a baby's coverlet.

BABY'S COVERLET

YOU WILL NEED

For the Coverlet, measuring 86cm × 104cm
(34in × 41in):

92cm × 110cm (37in × 44in) of Anne Afghan fabric
Stranded embroidery cotton in the colours given in
the panel
No26 tapestry needle
Matching sewing thread

•

THE EMBROIDERY

Following the diagram, cut the fabric to size. If you
are securing the fringe by machine, stitch a zigzag
border all around, as indicated. Mark the centre
lines of each design with basting stitches, and mount
the fabric in a hoop, following the instructions on
page 5. Referring to the appropriate chart, complete
each design, starting at the centre of each and using
two strands in the needle for the cross stitching, and
one for the backstitching.

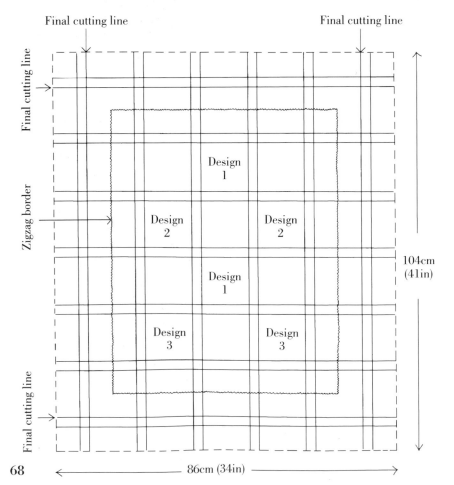

COMPLETING THE COVERLET

Trim the fabric to the final size. To make the fringe,
remove fabric threads one at a time until you reach
the zigzag stitch line. Brush out the fringe with a stiff
brush.

HEMSTITCH

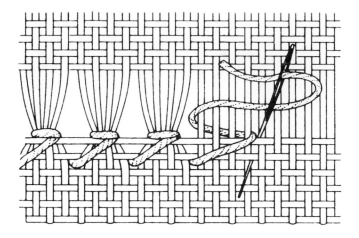

To finish with a traditional hem-stitched and fringed
edge, remove a single thread from the fabric at the
hem-line (the start of the fringe). Bring the needle
out on the right side, two threads below the drawn-
thread line. Working from left to right, pick up either
two or three threads, as shown in the diagram. Bring
the needle out again and insert it behind the fabric,
to emerge two threads down, ready to make the next
stitch. Before reinserting the needle, pull the thread
tight, so that the bound threads form a neat group. To
complete the fringe, remove the weft threads below
the hemstitching.

MUSICAL CLOWNS ▶	DMC	ANCHOR	MADEIRA
· White	White	2	White
⁄ Dark lemon yellow	444	291	0108
C Light steel grey	318	399	1808
O Tangerine orange	740	316	0202
■ Black	310	403	Black
● Bright Christmas red	666	46	0210
‖ Dark delft blue	798	131	0911
V Medium emerald green	911	205	1214

Note: bks with black.

Gifts for Children

Birthday and Christmas presents need no longer be a problem for sons, daughters, nieces and nephews. In this chapter there is something for every child, from toy bags to school bags and from finger puppets to bookmark baddies.

PRINCESS NOVELTY PICTURES

YOU WILL NEED

For each Picture set in a frame with an internal measurement of 8.5cm × 13.5cm (3½in × 5½in):

25cm × 20cm (10in × 8in) of white, 18-count Aida fabric
No26 tapestry needle
Stranded embroidery cotton in the colours given in the panel
Picture frame as specified above
Firm card to fit the frame

Lightweight synthetic batting/wadding, the same size as the card
Strong thread for mounting
Glue stick

NOTE: the same thread colours are used for both pictures; if you wish to embroider both designs, finish one picture and then decide whether you need any additional skeins before you start the next.

•

THE EMBROIDERY

Prepare the fabric as described on page 5; find the centre by folding the fabric in half and then in half again, and lightly pressing the folded corner, or by marking the horizontal and vertical centre lines with basting stitches in a light-coloured thread. Mount

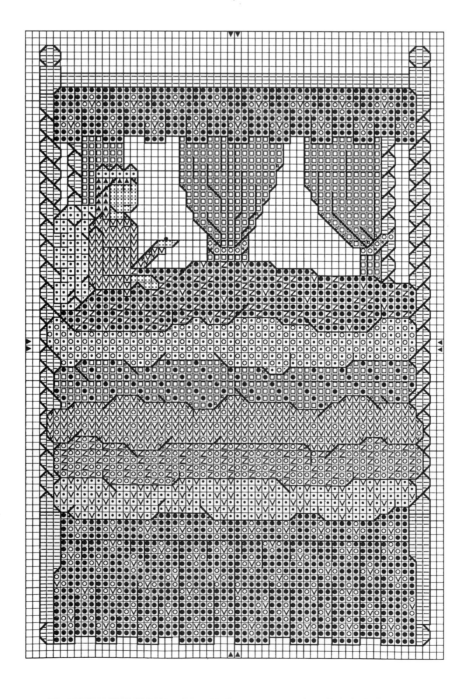

the fabric in a frame (see page 5), and start the design from the centre.

Following the chart, complete all the cross stitching first, using one strand of thread in the needle. These designs contain three-quarter stitches (see page 7), which are shown on the chart by the smaller symbols, and should be stitched in the corners indicated. Finish with the backstitching, again using one strand of thread. In the Princess picture, create the pea in the palm of her hand with one French knot, using three strands of thread in the needle.

Cut three lengths of medium brown thread approximately 30cm (12in) long. Knot the ends, and stitch each thread through the fabric at the base of the hair so that the knot is at the back of the work. Plait the threads: take the right-hand thread up and over the middle thread, which now becomes the middle thread; next, take the left-hand thread up and over the middle thread. By repeating this operation, plait to the end of the threads, then secure the ends by knotting.

MOUNTING AND FRAMING

Remove the finished embroidery from the frame and wash if necessary, then press lightly on the wrong side, using a steam iron. Spread glue evenly on one side of the mounting card and lightly press the batting/wadding to the surface. Lace the embroidery over the padded surface (see page 9), using the basting stitches (if any) to check that the embroidery is centred over the card. Remove basting stitches; coil the hair at the bottom of the picture, and place the mounted embroidery in the frame according to the manufacturer's instructions.

PRINCESS NOVELTY PICTURES ◀		ANCHOR	DMC	MADEIRA
•	Lemon yellow	301	744	0110
∷	Pale peach	8	754	0304
Z	Medium peach	9	352	0302
O	Deep pink	39	309	0507
▢	Pale blue	160	813	1002
●	Medium blue	146	798	0911
	Dark blue*	150	823	1007
V	Grass green	225	703	1307
—	Light brown	349	301	2306
▲	Medium brown	358	433	2008

Note: bks the outline with one strand of dark blue thread* (*used for backstitching only).

Genie School Bags

This delightful set of items – a gym bag, a pencil case, and a set of little novelty designs – all based on the story of Aladdin and his wondrous lamp, would make a lovely gift to celebrate a child's first day at school, or the start of a new year.

GENIE SCHOOL BAGS

YOU WILL NEED

For the Gym Bag, measuring 32cm × 45.5cm
(12½in × 18in):

23cm × 12.5cm (9in × 5in) of 14-count waste canvas
Stranded embroidery cotton in the colours given
in the panel
Sharp-pointed needle
66cm × 50.5cm (26in × 20in) of lightweight denim
Matching sewing cotton
1m (1yd) of medium-weight cord

For the Pencil Case, measuring approximately
16cm × 12cm (6½in × 4½in):

15cm × 10cm (6in × 4in) of 14-count waste canvas
Stranded embroidery cotton in the colours
given in the panel
Sharp-pointed needle
25cm × 20cm (10in × 8in) of lightweight denim
25cm × 20cm (10in × 8in) of pelmet-weight
interfacing
Matching sewing cotton
15cm (6in) jeans zip

For three Pencil-Case Novelties, each measuring
approximately 4.5cm × 2.5cm (1¾in × 1in):

10-count plastic canvas
Stranded embroidery cotton in the colours
given in the panel
No24 tapestry needle
Sticky-backed plastic
Strong thread, for ties

●

THE EMBROIDERY FOR GYM BAG AND PENCIL CASE

Fold the fabric for the gym bag in half to form a rectangle measuring 33cm × 50.5cm (13in × 20in) and
press. Unfold the fabric; place the waste canvas in
the middle of one half of the fabric, with the fold at
one side, and baste in position. For the pencil case
fold the fabric in half to form a rectangle measuring
20cm × 10cm (8in × 4in) and press. Unfold the fabric; place the waste canvas in the middle of the top
half of the fabric, with the fold at the bottom, and
baste in position.

Mount the fabric in a frame (see page 5) and start

the design in the middle, treating each pair of canvas threads as one. Following the chart, complete all
the cross stitching first, using three strands of thread
in a sharp-pointed needle. Finally, backstitch
around the outline, using two strands of royal blue
thread in the needle.

When you have finished the embroidery cut away
surplus canvas, leaving about 12mm (½in) of waste
canvas around the design. Dampen the right side
with slightly warm water and leave it for a few minutes until the sizing in the canvas softens. Gently
remove the canvas threads, one at a time, using
tweezers. The threads should come out easily, but
the operation requires patience; if you try to remove
several threads at once, this could spoil the embroidery. Finally, dry and press the work.

MAKING THE GYM BAG

Fold the fabric in half, with the embroidery on the
inside, and pin along the opposite edge to the fold
and across the bottom. Machine down the side and
along the bottom, 12mm (½in) from the edge, and
finish by overlocking the raw edges to stop the fabric
fraying. Fold the fabric at the top of the bag over to
the wrong side to form a 12mm (½in) turning and
press the fold. Fold the fabric again to form a 2.5cm
(1in) hem and machine along the bottom edge, leaving a 5cm (2in) opening at the seam. Insert the cord
and knot the ends together. Turn the bag right side
out and press to finish.

MAKING THE PENCIL CASE

Place the fabric, right side up, on the interfacing and
baste together. Place the zip, face down, along the
top edge of the fabric and machine in place. Place
the other side of the zip on the opposite edge and
machine – the work at this stage is inside out. Make
sure that the zip is open before pinning, then
machine down the sides of the case. Overlock the
sides to stop the fabric fraying. Turn the case right
side out and finish by pressing.

PENCIL CASE NOVELTIES

Following the chart, cross stitch, using six strands of
thread in the needle. Do not take threads from one
design to another as the stitching may unravel when
the canvas is separated. Backstitch, using six
strands of thread, in the background colour chosen.
Trim away surplus canvas by cutting into the first set
of empty holes around the design. Do not cut into
embroidered holes. Overcast the plastic around the
design in the background colour, using all six

strands of thread. Finally, stick a small square of sticky-backed plastic on the wrong side of the canvas and carefully trim to fit the shape. Attach the motif by a strong thread, laced through the top of the lamp, to the object required.

GENIE SCHOOL MOTIFS	ANCHOR	DMC	MADEIRA
⊡ White	1	White	White
⊟ Lemon yellow	288	445	0103
⊠ Golden yellow	291	444	0106
⊙ Pink	54	956	0611
⊟ Spring green	226	702	1306
⬤ Royal blue	133	796	0913

Note: bks around outline, using two strands of royal blue thread in the needle.

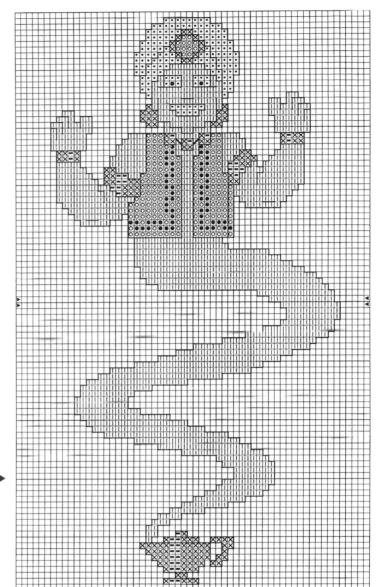

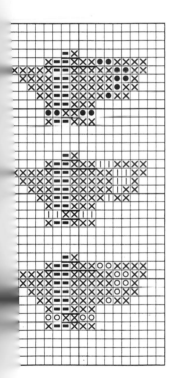

◀ PENCIL CASE
NOVELTIES

GYM BAG ▶

▼ PENCIL CASE

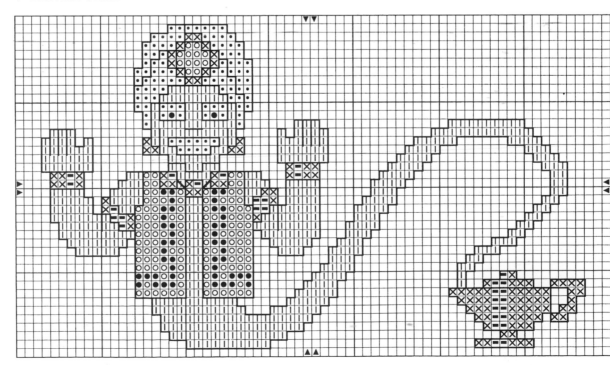

Jack & the Beanstalk Wall Chart

Stitch this chart and watch your child grow up to the giant's castle. The chart reaches 100cm (39³⁄₈in) but you could change the measurements for an older child.

100

90

80

70

60

50

40

JACK & THE BEANSTALK WALL CHART

YOU WILL NEED

For the Wall Chart, measuring 69cm × 15cm (27in × 6in) approximately:

78.5cm × 22.5cm (31in × 9in) of cream, 11-count Aida fabric
74cm × 20cm (29in × 8in) of cream cotton fabric, for backing
Stranded cottons in the colours given in the appropriate panel
No24 tapestry needle
Cream sewing cotton
Wall hanging rods for a hanging 15cm (6in) wide, for suppliers see page 256

THE EMBROIDERY

Prepare the fabric as described on page 5; find the centre by folding the fabric in half and then in half again, and lightly pressing the folded corner, or by marking the horizontal and vertical centre lines with basting stitches in a light-coloured thread. Mount the fabric in a frame (see page 5) and start the embroidery by stitching the measurements on the left-hand side of the design. These must be stitched carefully as the number of squares between the marks changes at 10cm intervals; this is an adjustment to improve the accuracy of the measurement chart.

Following the chart, complete the measurement marks first, using three strands of thread in the needle. Continue with the cross stitching, again using three strands of thread in the needle. This design contains three-quarter stitches (see page 7), which are shown on the chart by the smaller symbols, and should be stitched in the corners indicated. Take care not to take dark threads across the back of the

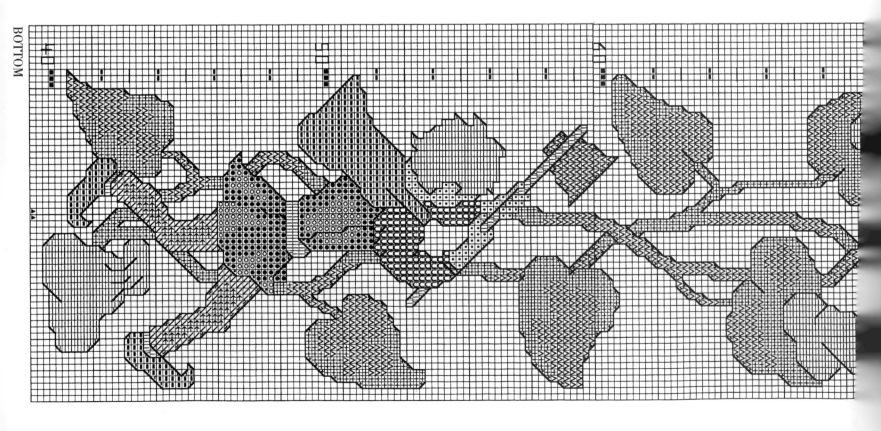

work in such a way that they show through on the right side. Backstitch the outline, using two strands of navy blue in the needle.

MAKING THE HANGING

Remove the finished embroidery from the frame and wash if necessary, then press lightly on the wrong side, using a steam iron. Keeping the embroidery centred, trim the Aida fabric to the same measurement as the backing fabric. Place the embroidery and backing fabric with right sides together and pin. Baste and then machine stitch down the length of the fabric on each side (you should have an allowance of five clear squares down each side between the stitching line and the embroidered area). Turn the work right side out and press.

To make the folds for the bell pull, overlock the Aida and backing fabric together at each end. Make a 2.5cm (1in) turning to the back of the work at both the top and bottom of the hanging. Machine stitch the hem approximately 6mm (¼in) from the turned edge. Insert the rods and assemble according to the manufacturer's instructions.

JACK & THE BEANSTALK ▼		ANCHOR	DMC	MADEIRA
V	Grey	848	927	1708
Y	Medium rose	68	3688	0604
⌐	Deep rose	69	3687	0603
▢	Light blue	161	826	1012
■	Medium blue	162	825	1011
	Navy blue*	150	823	1008
←	Pale orange	302	743	0113
⟍	Orange	303	742	0114
—	Bronze	309	781	2009
⏐	Medium brown	357	801	2302
·	Peach	6	754	0305
▬	Red	13	349	0212
U	Light lilac	108	210	0801
O	Medium lilac	98	553	0803
●	Medium purple	111	208	0804
∧	Light green	226	702	1306
+	Medium green	230	910	1301

Note: where small symbol is shown, work a three-quarter stitch in the corner indicated; bks around the outline with two strands of navy blue (*used for backstitching only).*

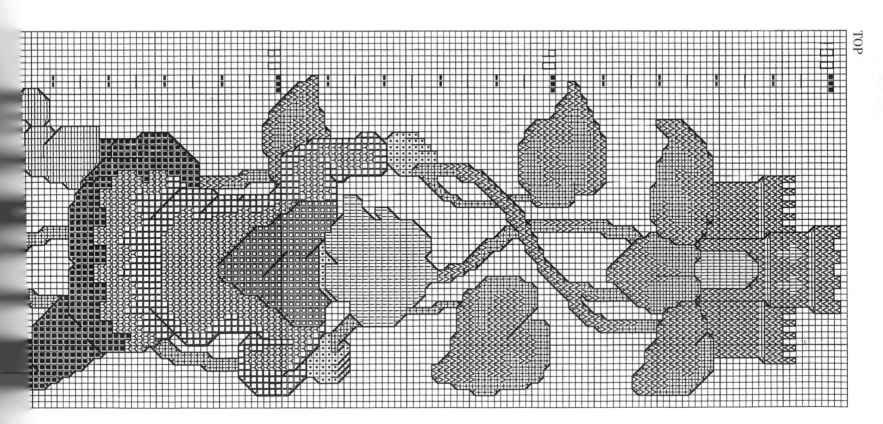

work in such a way that they show through on the right side. Backstitch the outline, using two strands of navy blue in the needle.

MAKING THE HANGING

Remove the finished embroidery from the frame and wash if necessary, then press lightly on the wrong side, using a steam iron. Keeping the embroidery centred, trim the Aida fabric to the same measurement as the backing fabric. Place the embroidery and backing fabric with right sides together and pin. Baste and then machine stitch down the length of the fabric on each side (you should have an allowance of five clear squares down each side between the stitching line and the embroidered area). Turn the work right side out and press.

To make the folds for the bell pull, overlock the Aida and backing fabric together at each end. Make a 2.5cm (1in) turning to the back of the work at both the top and bottom of the hanging. Machine stitch the hem approximately 6mm (¼in) from the turned edge. Insert the rods and assemble according to the manufacturer's instructions.

JACK & THE BEANSTALK ▼		ANCHOR	DMC	MADEIRA
V	Grey	848	927	1708
Y	Medium rose	68	3688	0604
˥	Deep rose	69	3687	0603
□	Light blue	161	826	1012
■	Medium blue	162	825	1011
	Navy blue*	150	823	1008
←	Pale orange	302	743	0113
＼	Orange	303	742	0114
▬	Bronze	309	781	2009
╎	Medium brown	357	801	2302
·	Peach	6	754	0305
▬	Red	13	349	0212
U	Light lilac	108	210	0801
O	Medium lilac	98	553	0803
●	Medium purple	111	208	0804
Λ	Light green	226	702	1306
+	Medium green	230	910	1301

Note: where small symbol is shown, work a three-quarter stitch in the corner indicated; bks around the outline with two strands of navy blue* (*used for backstitching only).

TOP

Snow White Party Crackers

Filled with a cracker and a small gift of your choice, these are ideal for children's birthday parties or Christmas treats, and if you wash them carefully, they can be re-used.

SNOW WHITE PARTY CRACKERS

YOU WILL NEED

For the complete set of eight Crackers:

One sheet of 10-count plastic canvas
*Stranded embroidery cotton in the colours given
in the panel*
No24 tapestry needle
*50cm (¹/₂yd) of cotton fabric, 90cm (1yd) wide, in
each of two contrasting colours*
*Sewing threads to match the fabrics and the
zigzag braid (see below)*
50cm (¹/₂yd) of interfacing (pelmet weight)
*80cm (30in) of ribbon, 2.5cm (1in) wide, in each of
two contrasting colours to match the fabrics*
*3.1m (3¹/₂yds) of ribbon, 3mm (¹/₈in) wide, in each of
the same two colours as above*
1.6m (1²/₃yds) of zigzag braid
1m (1yd) of iron-on Velcro, 2cm (³/₄in) wide
*Eight cardboard tubes, each 10cm (4in) long and
4cm (1¹/₂in) in diameter (toilet roll centres are ideal)*
Fillings of your choice

NOTE: *cut the Velcro down the centre, to create two
1m (1yd) lengths.*

Using the above cut, for each cracker, measuring approximately 23.5cm in length × 4.5cm in diameter (9¹/₄in × 1³/₄in):

31.5cm × 19cm (12¹/₂in × 7¹/₂in) of cotton fabric
*Interfacing – two 16cm × 5.5cm (6¹/₂in × 2¹/₄in)
pieces, and one 16cm × 11cm (6¹/₂in × 4¹/₄in) piece*
*Velcro – one 2.5cm (1in) length, two 5cm (2in)
lengths and one 10cm (4in) length*
*Wide ribbon – 19cm (7¹/₂in), to contrast with
the fabric*
*Narrow ribbon – two 38cm (15in) lengths, to
contrast with the fabric*

•

THE EMBROIDERY

Work all the figures before attempting to cut the canvas, as cutting errors cannot be rectified. Remember to leave at least one space between designs for cutting. Follow the chart and cross stitch, using all six strands of thread in the needle; do not take threads from one design to another as the stitching may unravel when the motifs are separated. Finally, backstitch the eyes and mouths, again using all six strands of thread.

Cut away surplus canvas carefully, the cutting line being the first empty square around the embroidery; do not cut into an embroidered square. Each figure will be left with a plastic ridge around the perimeter; simply overcast this in the light brown thread, still using all six strands in the needle.

MAKING THE CRACKERS

For each cracker, take a piece of cotton fabric and lay a smaller-sized piece of interfacing on the right side at one end, with long edges matching and an even overlap of fabric at the sides. Taking a 6mm (¹/₄in) allowance, machine the two together down the long edge. Bring the fabric over the interfacing (folding the fabric only to create a 6mm/¹/₄in hem of fabric at the wrong side) and machine the two together along the other long edge. Repeat this operation at the other end of the cracker. Position the larger piece of interfacing on the centre of the fabric (wrong side), and machine along the two long edges.

Turn to the right side of the fabric, and machine a length of zigzag braid to each end, approximately 2.5cm (1in) from the folded edge. Place a contrast strip of wide ribbon across the centre of the fabric and stitch the ribbon to the fabric down each long edge, either slipstitching neatly and unobtrusively by hand or with machine stitching.

Turn a double 6mm (¹/₄in) hem to the wrong side down each long edge of the cracker, and neatly slipstitch in place.

Separate the three longer Velcro strips and place the hooked sections on the inside edge (over the hem and interfacing); the corresponding pieces go on the outside of the fabric down the opposite edge, so that when the fabric is wrapped around the cardboard tube, the strips will interlock. Use the diagram to check that the strips are correctly placed, before ironing them in position. Finally, machine them to secure them in position.

Thread narrow ribbon into a large-eyed sharp needle and stitch it exactly in between the interfacing pieces at each side of the centre strip, to create the ribbon ties at each end of the cracker. Take the remaining, short piece of Velcro and stitch one side down the back of a canvas motif and the other section down the centre of the cracker, across the ribbon.

Place the cardboard tube, and fillings of your choice, at the centre back of the cracker; close the strips; draw up the ribbon ties; tie a bow at each end, and lightly press the motif to the centre of the cracker.

It is important to stitch the iron-on Velcro securely to the fabric and motif as young children cannot be expected to handle these crackers gently. To wash the crackers, simply remove the motifs and wash in the normal way. The canvas motifs can be washed by hand but should not be ironed.

SNOW WHITE AND THE SEVEN DWARFS		ANCHOR	DMC	MADEIRA
‖	Cream	275	712	2101
·	Light peach	6	754	0502
∷	Medium peach	8	353	0503
+	Gold	306	725	0113
╱	Light brown	374	420	2104
Y	Medium brown	358	433	2008
■	Dark brown	381	938	2005
○	Red	46	666	0210
●	Dark red	43	816	0512
↓	Yellow green	279	734	1610
3	Grass green	255	907	1410
X	Dark green	246	986	1405
◆	Royal blue	133	796	0913

Note: stitch the eyes in royal blue and mouths in red.

RIGHT SIDE

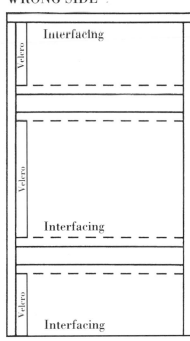

WRONG SIDE

SNOW WHITE

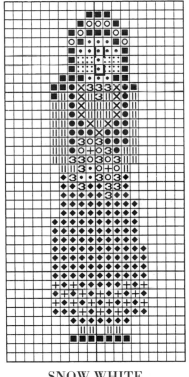

Nightdress Case

Make this colourful nightdress case to tuck away your child's nightie or pyjamas during the day. Lightly padded, trimmed with ribbon bows, and featuring an acrobatic clown doing the splits, it will brighten up any bedroom.

NIGHTDRESS CASE

YOU WILL NEED

For the Nightdress Case, measuring
45cm × 33cm (17³/₄in × 13in):

*94cm × 47.5cm (37in × 18³/₄in) of sky blue,
14-count Aida fabric
Stranded embroidery cotton in the colours given
in the panel
No24 tapestry needle
Sewing thread to match the fabric
94cm × 47.5cm (37in × 18³/₄in) of lightweight
polyester batting
94cm × 47.5cm (37in × 18³/₄in) of lightweight
cotton fabric for the lining
1.12m (44in) of ribbon, 2.5cm (1in) wide,
in a contrasting colour*

●

THE EMBROIDERY

Prepare the edges of the fabric (see page 5); baste a
line across the width, 7.5cm (3in) up from the
bottom edge, to mark the baseline of the embroidery,
and another 28.5cm (11¹/₂in) up from the bottom
edge (this marks off the area for the front flap), then
baste horizontal and vertical lines across the embroidery area.

Complete the cross stitching, working from the
centre and using two strands of embroidery thread in
the needle. Finish with the backstitching, using one
strand of thread in the needle. Gently steam press
the embroidery from the wrong side.

MAKING THE NIGHTDRESS CASE

Place the embroidered fabric face down on a flat
surface; carefully smooth the batting on top; pin and
baste the two together (12mm/¹/₂in seam allowance);
trim the batting back almost to the basting line, and
catch-stitch around the edge.

Make a single 12mm (¹/₂in) turning across the
width (not flap edge) of the fabric and baste. With
right sides facing, fold the pocket front section over
for 32cm (12¹/₂in); baste, and machine stitch to form
the pocket. Trim the corners and turn right side out.

Make a single turning on the short edge of the
lining fabric and repeat as for the top fabric, but do
not turn the pocket to the right side.

With right sides of the top fabric and lining
together, baste and stitch around the flap, finishing

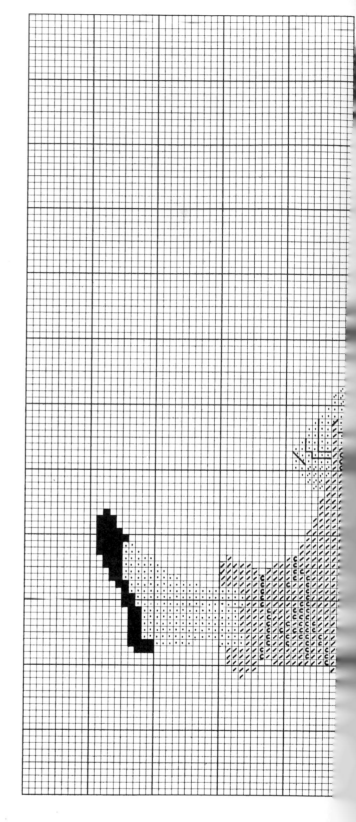

just above the side seams. Trim the corners and turn
the flap through to the right side. Slip the lining into
the pocket and slipstitch the top edges together,
easing the turning so that the stitching is on the
inside. Remove the basting stitches.

Cut the ribbon into two equal lengths; make two
bows and catch-stitch them to the flap of the nightdress case diagonally across the corners, as shown in
the photograph.

THE SPLITS ▲	DMC	ANCHOR	MADEIRA			DMC	ANCHOR	MADEIRA
C Deep canary yellow	972	303	0107	‖ Dark violet		552	100	0713
= Pale grey	415	398	1803	X Medium garnet red		815	43	0513
● Very dark violet	550	101	0714	○ Bright orange red		606	335	0209
· Christmas red	321	47	0510	Light steel grey*		318	399	1808
6 Medium delft blue	799	130	0910					
/ Dark lemon yellow	444	291	0108					
■ Black	310	403	Black					
· White	White	2	White					

Note: bks using light steel grey* (*used for bks only) for hands and face, and black for eyes and eyebrows.

Red Riding Hood Finger Puppets

Stitch these colourful finger puppets
and bring to life a favourite story.
This charming set would be an ideal
gift to bring some drama and
excitement to a convalescent child.

RED RIDING HOOD FINGER PUPPETS

YOU WILL NEED

For six Finger Puppets, each measuring approximately 7.5cm × 4cm (3in × 1½in):

40cm × 20cm (16in × 8in) of white, 14-count Aida fabric
40cm × 20cm (16in × 8in) of cotton fabric
Stranded embroidery cotton in the colours given in the panel
No26 tapestry needle
Sewing cotton to match fabric

•

THE EMBROIDERY

Using a light-coloured thread, baste six boxes, each with a count of twenty horizontal squares by eighty vertical squares. Position the boxes side by side, as shown in the diagram, with an allowance of five squares between each. Mount the Aida fabric in a hoop or frame (see pages 5 and 6). If you wish to work in a hoop, you may need a larger piece of Aida fabric or additional strips to increase the size of the fabric.

Embroider one figure in each of the six boxes, placing each design in the top forty squares of a rectangular box. Following the appropriate chart, complete all the cross stitching, using two strands of thread in the needle. These designs contain three-quarter stitches (see page 7) which are shown on the chart by the smaller symbols; and should be stitched in the corners indicated. Do not take threads from one design to another as the stitching may unravel when the embroideries are separated. Backstitch the eyes with three strands of navy thread in the needle; alternatively you may prefer to use french knots. The main outline of each design should be backstitched with one strand of navy thread.

MAKING THE FINGER PUPPETS

Take the finished embroidery from the frame; wash if necessary, and press lightly with a steam iron. Do not remove the basting stitches around the boxes as these will be used as guidelines for the machining. Place the cotton backing fabric and the Aida together, right sides facing, and pin around the perimeter.

Machine around three sides of each puppet (two sides and the top), leaving the bottom unstitched; to do this, use the basting stitches as guidelines, and machine outside the boxes, approximately one square away from the basted line. Machine around all six boxes before dividing the puppets.

To separate, cut between the stitched puppets, taking care not to trim too close to the stitching. Trim away any surplus material and overlock the edges to prevent fraying.

Turn the puppets inside out. This will need to be done very carefully – try not to pull on the embroideries. You will find a blunt object, such as the end of a pen, useful for pushing out the corners. Remove any creases by pressing, then overlock the open end. Finally, push the overlocked end up and into the top to form the lining.

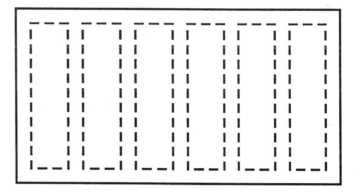

Marking out the embroidery fabric

RED RIDING HOOD FINGER PUPPETS ►		ANCHOR	DMC	MADEIRA
⊘	Yellow	305	743	0113
▲	Orange	303	741	0114
·	Pale peach	6	754	0304
∷	Medium peach	9	353	0303
○	Red	335	606	0209
X	Green	255	907	1410
◇	Blue	145	799	1003
●	Brown	359	898	2006
─	Grey	848	928	1708
	Navy blue*	150	823	1008

Note: bks the outline around each design in navy blue* (*used for backstitching only), and stitch the mouths of Red Riding Hood, Grandma and the Woodcutter in red, using one strand in the needle.

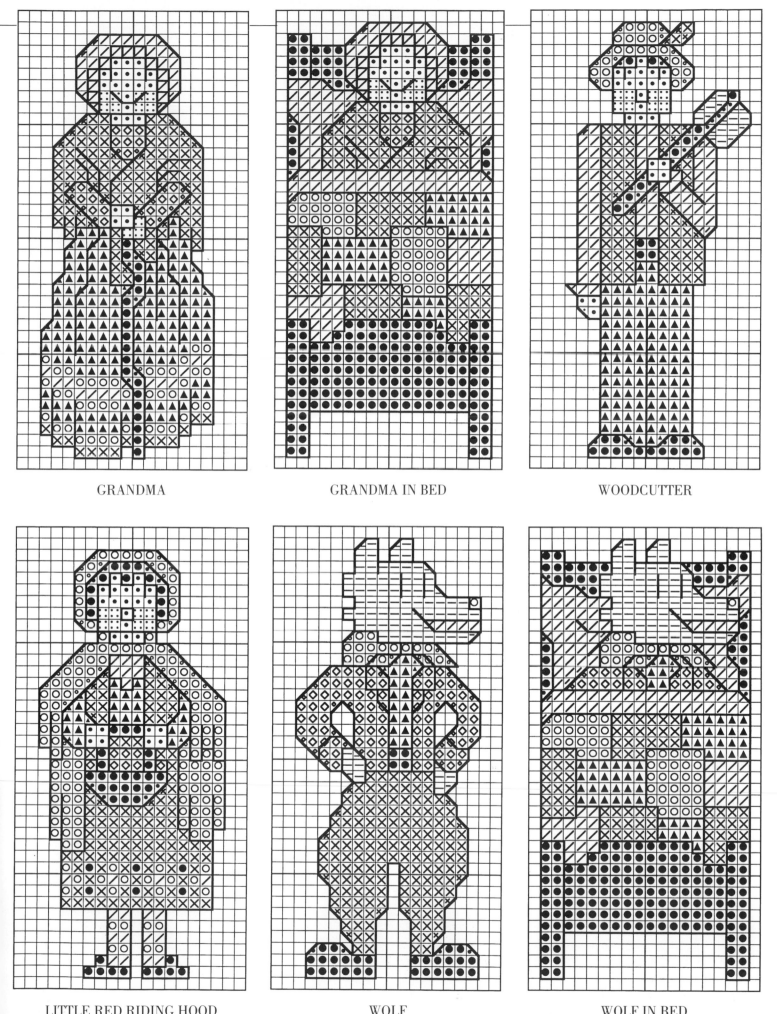

GRANDMA   GRANDMA IN BED   WOODCUTTER

LITTLE RED RIDING HOOD   WOLF   WOLF IN BED

Bookmark Baddies

Here is a set of characters that children love to hate. A hand-stitched bookmark baddy would make the perfect small token to be slipped inside a birthday card or used as a parting gift after a Hallowe'en party.

BOOKMARK BADDIES

YOU WILL NEED

For each Bookmark, measuring 23cm × 5cm
(9in × 2in), including the fringe:

*33cm × 22.5cm (13in × 9in) of white,
14-count Aida fabric
Stranded embroidery cotton in the colours given
in the appropriate panel
No26 tapestry needle
Sewing cotton to match the fabric*

NOTE: *one skein of each colour on the combined list
is sufficient for all three designs. The fabric quantity
quoted above includes an allowance of 10cm (4in)
each way, for framing; if you are making more than
one bookmark, allow 23cm × 12.5cm (9in × 5in) for
each, plus a 5cm (2in) margin around the total area.*

•

THE EMBROIDERY

Prepare the fabric as described on page 5; find the
centre by folding the fabric in half and then in half
again, and lightly pressing the folded corner, or by
marking the horizontal and vertical centre lines with
basting stitches in a light-coloured thread. If you are
stitching two or more designs at once, separate the
bookmark areas 23cm x 12.5cm (9in x 5in) with
lines of basting stitches, and mark the centre of each
area, but do not cut them apart until you have finished the embroidery. Mount the prepared fabric in a
hoop or frame (see page 5).

Following the chart, complete all the cross
stitching, using two strands of thread in the needle.
These designs contain three-quarter stitches (see
page 7), which are shown on the chart by the smaller
symbols, and should be stitched in the corners indicated. Finish with the backstitching. Use one strand
of black thread in the needle for the outline. Finally,
stitch the stars with two strands of golden yellow
thread in the needle, making each side of each star
with one long single stitch.

MAKING THE BOOKMARK

Remove the finished embroidery from the frame. If
you are making several bookmarks trim away the
5cm (2in) margin around the total area, and cut the
embroideries apart along the basted dividing lines; if
you are making one bookmark only, trim the fabric to
the correct size – 23cm × 12.5cm (9in × 5in).

Fray the top and bottom of fabric by removing
horizontal threads, leaving about 2cm (³/₄in) of vertical threads showing. Oversew the fabric at the base
of the frayed edges with matching sewing cotton to
prevent further fraying. Fold the fabric down each
side of the work to the back, leaving about 3mm
(¹/₈in) clearance each side of the embroidery, and
press the folds lightly with a steam iron. At the back
of the work, place one flap over the other, turning in
a small seam down the overlapping edge, and finish
by hemming the length of the bookmark.

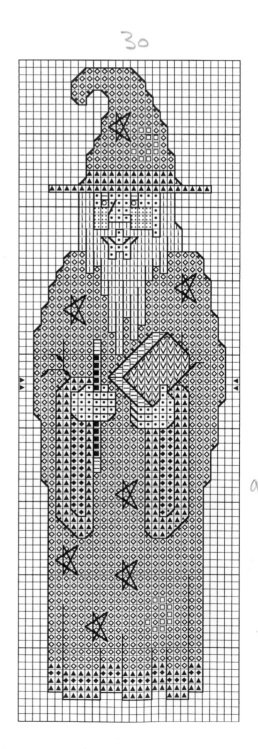

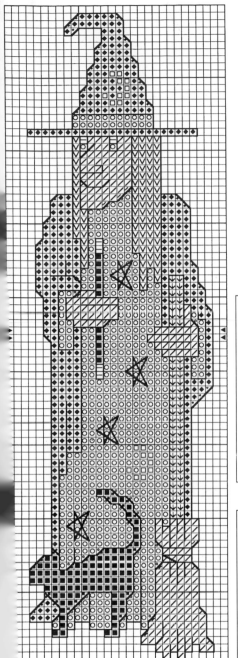

ALL THREE DESIGNS		ANCHOR	DMC	MADEIRA
⊟	White	1	White	White
⊡	Grey	397	453	1805
▢	Golden yellow	302	743	0113
↓	Light brown	349	301	2306
·	Pale peach	6	754	0304
∷	Medium peach	9	353	0303
X	Rose red	39	309	0507
◆	Plum	69	3685	0602
◿	Apple green	240	368	1604
V	Medium green	230	910	1301
●	Dark green	862	520	1506
○	Blue	137	797	1004
◇	Lilac	98	553	0711
▲	Purple	101	550	0712
■	Black	403	Black	Black

WITCH ◄		ANCHOR	DMC	MADEIRA
⊟	White	1	White	White
▢	Golden yellow	302	743	0113
◿	Apple green	240	368	1604
V	Medium green	230	910	1301
○	Blue	137	797	1004
◆	Plum	69	3685	0602
↓	Light brown	349	301	2306
■	Black	403	Black	Black

Note: bks around the outline in black and the stars in golden yellow.

SORCERER ▶		ANCHOR	DMC	MADEIRA
⊟	White	1	White	White
⊡	Grey	397	453	1805
▢	Golden yellow	302	743	0113
·	Pale peach	6	754	0304
∷	Medium peach	9	353	0303
X	Rose red	39	309	0507
◿	Apple green	240	368	1604
●	Dark green	862	520	1506
○	Blue	137	797	1004
■	Black	403	Black	Black

Note: bks around the outline in black and the stars in golden yellow.

IZARD ◄	ANCHOR	DMC	MADEIRA
White	1	White	White
Grey	397	453	1805
Golden yellow	302	743	0113
Pale peach	6	754	0304
Medium peach	9	353	0303
Medium green	230	910	1301
Blue	137	797	1004
Lilac	98	553	0711
Purple	101	550	0712
Plum	69	3685	0602
Black	403	Black	Black

te: bks around the outline in black and the stars in golden low.

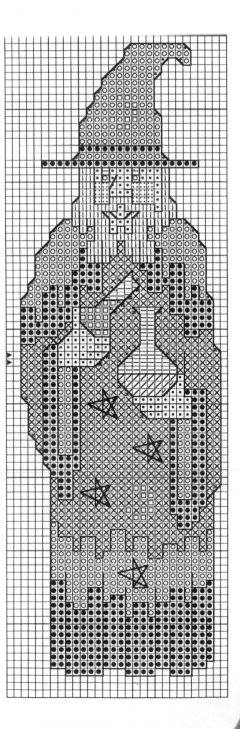

Clown Toy Bag

Suitable for a child of any age, this toy bag will make an extremely practical gift, and a bright and attractive feature in the playroom or nursery. The bag has a drawstring top and is both large and strong enough to hold many small toys.

CLOWN TOY BAG

YOU WILL NEED

For a Toy Bag, measuring 48cm × 35.5cm
(19in × 14in):

*50.5cm × 38cm (20in × 15in) of white pearl,
11-count Aida fabric
Stranded embroidery cotton in the colours given in
the panel
Matching sewing thread
No24 tapestry needle
Three pieces of white cotton fabric, each measuring
50.5cm × 38cm (20in × 15in), for the backing
and lining
2.5m (2¹/₂yd) of white cord, 6mm (¹/₄in)
in diameter*

●

THE EMBROIDERY

Prepare the Aida fabric, marking the centre lines of the design with basting stitches; ensure that there is a clearance around the design area of 9cm (3¹/₂in) at the sides, and 6.5cm (2¹/₂in) at the bottom. Mount it in a hoop or frame, following the instructions on page 5. Referring to the chart, complete the cross stitching, using three strands in the needle. Embroider the main area first, then finish with the backstitching, using two strands of thread in the needle. Steam press on the wrong side.

MAKING THE BAG

Place the Aida and one piece of the white cotton fabric right sides together. Taking a 12mm (¹/₂in) seam allowance, stitch the side seams down from the top for 4cm (1¹/₂in). Leave a gap of 2.5cm (1in), then recommence stitching the side seams to the bottom, as shown in diagram A.

Press the side seams open around the gap and top stitch 6mm (¹/₄in) from the edge, as shown in diagram B. Stitch the bottom seam. Turn to the right side and press, trying not to iron over the embroidery.

Place the two remaining pieces of cotton fabric right sides together, and stitch the side seams. Stitch the bottom seam, leaving an opening of 10cm (4in) for turning inside out (see diagram C). *Do not turn yet.*

Place the outer bag into the lining, with right

sides together, and stitch around the top edge. Turn right side out, easing through the opening at the bottom of the lining. Hand-stitch the lining together at the bottom.

Press the top edge of the bag along the seam. Topstitch around the bag 6mm (¹/₄in) above the cord opening and again 6mm (¹/₄in) below, as shown in diagram D. Thread the cord twice through the casement made by the two rows of stitches, and tie the ends together.

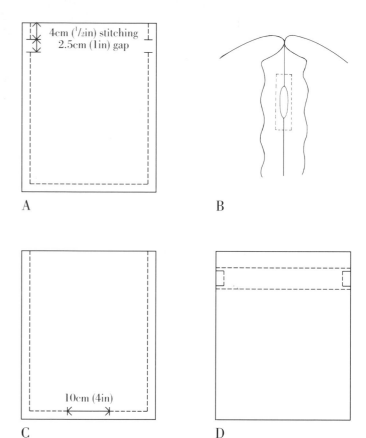

CLOWN TOY BAG ▶		DMC	ANCHOR	MADEIRA
II	Light cranberry	604	305	0504
／	Light emerald green	912	209	1212
■	Black	310	403	Black
∴	Off white	746	386	0101
X	Lemon yellow	307	289	0104
·	White	White	2	White
●	Bright Christmas red	666	46	0210
○	Bright orange	608	333	0206
=	Tan brown	436	363	2011
V	Pale grey	415	398	1803

Note: bks with black.

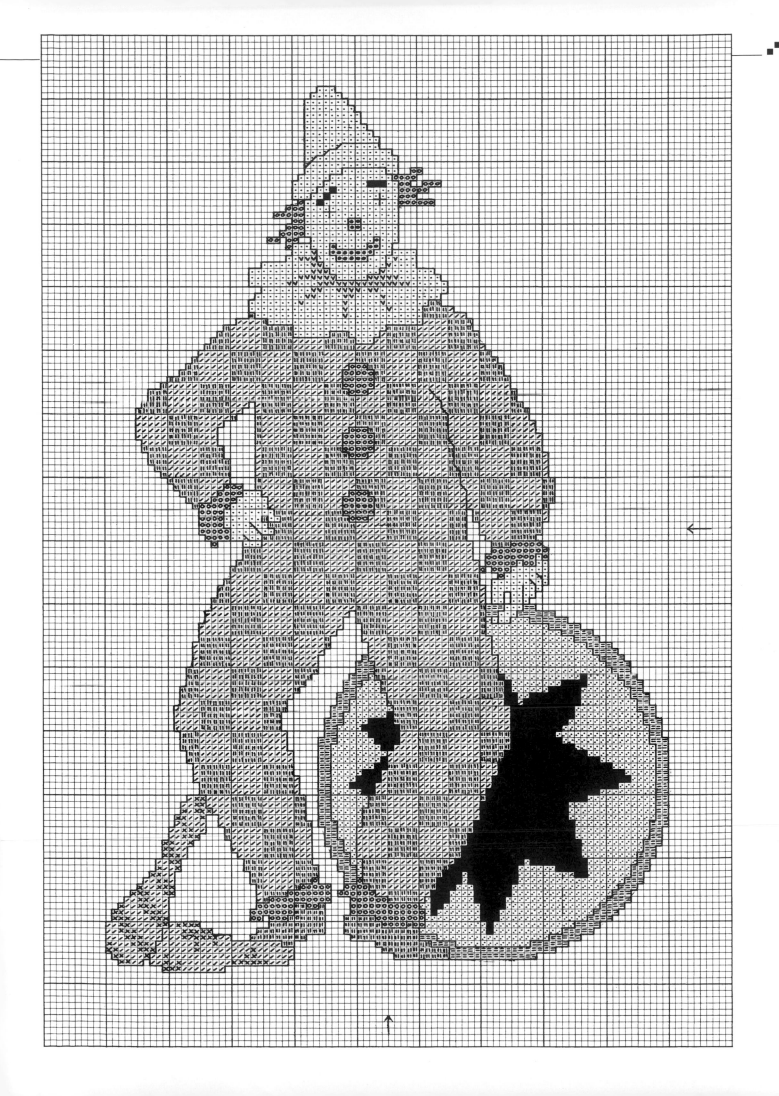

101

SAMPLERS

This chapter will delight all stitchers who love the elegance of a sampler. Some of the designs are traditional, while others have a more contemporary style, and any of them could be adapted to make miniature pictures or cushion covers to complement your sampler. You could even use these designs as starting points for creating your own personal sampler.

WEDDING SAMPLER AND BRIDE'S TOKEN

YOU WILL NEED

For the Wedding Sampler, with a design area measuring 20cm (7³⁄₄ in) square or 88 stitches by 88 stitches, here in a frame measuring 27cm (10³⁄₄ in) square:

30cm (11³⁄₄ in) square of white, 11-count Aida fabric
Stranded embroidery cotton in the colours given in the appropriate panel
Silver thread (DMC code 278, shade 4041)
No24 tapestry needle
Strong thread, for lacing across the back
Cardboard, for mounting
Frame of your choice

For the Bride's Token, with a design area measuring 9.5cm × 7.5cm (3³⁄₄ in × 3 in):

13cm × 11cm (5 in × 4¹⁄₄ in) of white, 14-count perforated paper
Stranded embroidery cotton in the colours given in the appropriate panel
Silver thread (DMC code 278, shade 4041)
No24 tapestry needle
14cm (5¹⁄₂ in) of pink ribbon, 6mm (¹⁄₄ in) wide
Fabric glue
13cm × 11cm (5 in × 4¹⁄₄ in) of white felt

•

WEDDING SAMPLER

Prepare the fabric and stretch it in a frame as explained on page 5. Following the chart, start the embroidery at the centre of the design using three strands of cotton in the needle or a 100cm (40in) length of silver thread folded double for the cross stitch. Work each stitch over one block of fabric in each direction. Make sure that all the top crosses run in the same direction and that each row is worked into the same holes as the row before so that you do not leave a space between the rows. Embroider the names and date in backstitch, referring to the alphabet chart and using two strands of cotton in the needle.

Gently press the finished embroidery on the **wrong side and mount it as explained on page 9. Choose a mount and frame to complement your** embroidery colours.

BRIDE'S TOKEN

Mark the centre of the perforated paper with a line of horizontal and vertical basting stitches. Following the chart, start the embroidery at the centre of the design using two strands of cotton in the needle or a 100cm (40in) length of silver thread folded double for the cross stitch. Handle the perforated paper carefully when sewing and ensure that you do not leave a long length of cotton at the back as this will show through. Work each stitch over one block of the paper in each direction. Work the backstitch using two strands of cotton in the needle.

Very carefully, cut around the tree about one square away from the embroidery. Do not cut too close as you will cut your stitches. Fold the ribbon in half and glue it to the wrong side of the tree at the top. Glue the tree to the piece of white felt and trim the excess felt away around the edge.

BRIDE'S TOKEN ▼		DMC	ANCHOR	MADEIRA
X	Light green	368	0214	1310
=	Dark green	320	0215	1311
O	Light pink	963	048	0608
+	Dark pink	3326	026	0504
	Grey*	414	0399	1801
S	Silver	Available from DMC only		
		Code 278, shade 4041		

Note: bks the boughs of the tree in dark green and the initials in grey (*used for backstitch only).*

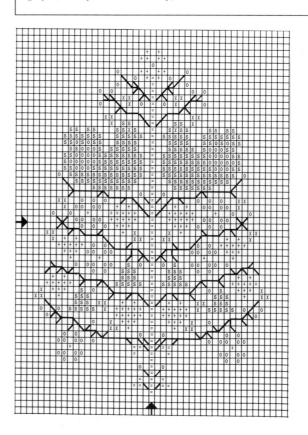

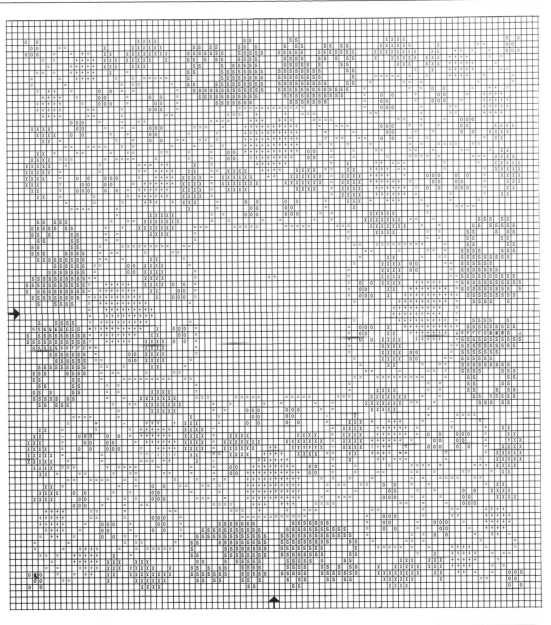

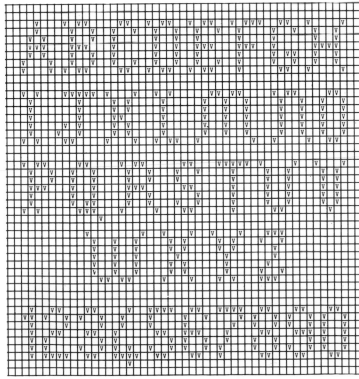

WEDDING SAMPLER ▲		DMC	ANCHOR	MADEIRA
X	Light green	368	0214	1310
=	Dark green	320	0215	1311
O	Light pink	963	048	0608
+	Dark pink	3326	026	0504
	Grey*	414	0399	1801
S	Silver	Available from DMC only Code 278, shade 4041		

Note: bks names and date in grey (*used for backstitch only).*

Farmyard Sampler

Combining tradition with modern design, this pretty little sampler really is the 'ABC' of the farm, the subtle sage green fabric complementing the bright colours. The motifs could be used on linen, greetings cards or children's clothes.

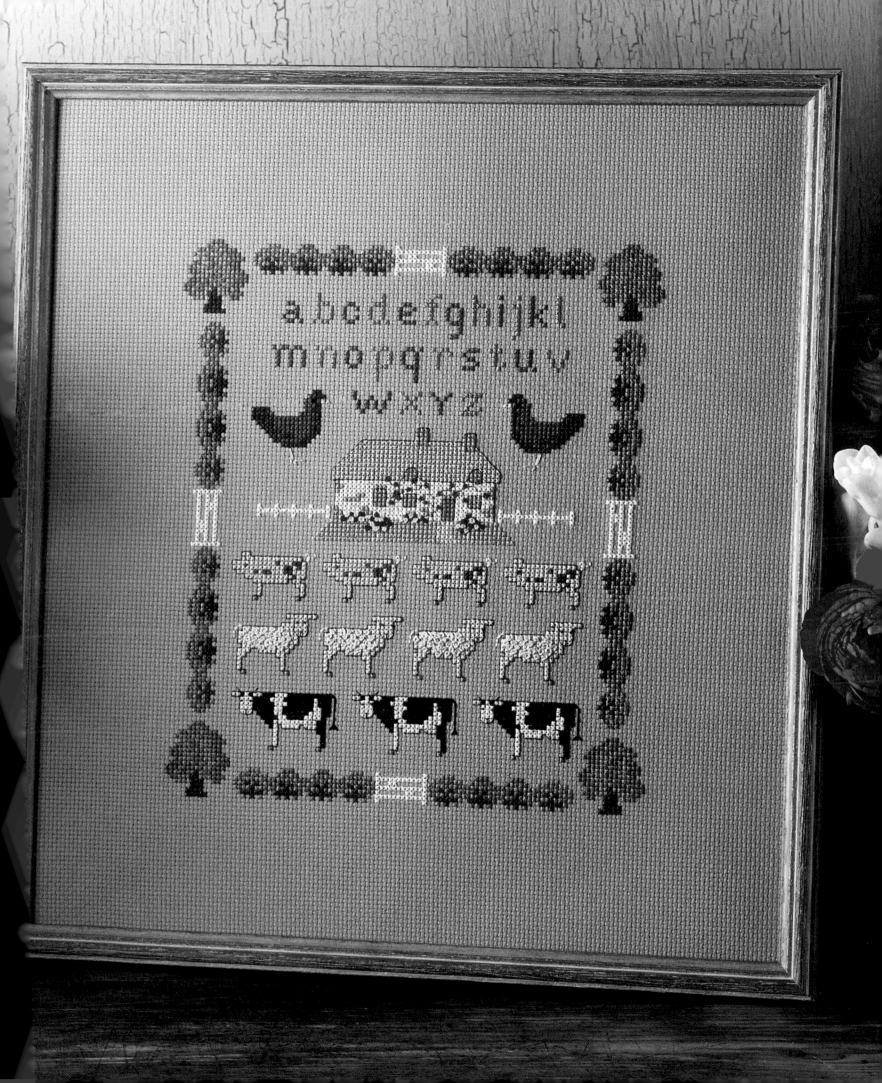

FARMYARD SAMPLER

YOU WILL NEED

For the Sampler, with a design area measuring
20cm × 23.5cm (8in × 9¹/₄in), here set in a frame
with an internal measurement of 31.5cm × 35.5cm
(12¹/₂in × 14in):

*44cm × 47cm (17¹/₂in × 18¹/₂in) of sage green,
14-count Aida fabric
Stranded embroidery cotton in the colours given
in the panel
No24 tapestry needle
Frame, as specified above
Strong thread and cardboard, for mounting*

•

THE EMBROIDERY

Prepare the fabric as described on page 5; find
the centre by folding, and mark the horizontal and
vertical centre lines with basting stitches in a light-
coloured thread. Set the fabric in a frame (see page
5) and count out from the centre to start stitching at
a point convenient to you.

Complete the cross stitching, using two strands of
thread in the needle and making sure that all top
stitches run in the same direction. Continue with the
backstitching, this time using one strand only for all
backstitching in dark grey and rich green, and two
strands for backstitching in fawn, pink, ecru and
black. Finish with french knots; the large knots that
make the flowers on the farmhouse and the fleecy
coats of the sheep are worked with two strands and
are indicated on the chart by circles, each enclosing
a graph intersection. The eyes of the pigs, sheep and
cows are also made with french knots, this time
worked with one strand only.

FINISHING

Remove the sampler from the frame. Gently
handwash the finished piece, if necessary, and
lightly press with a steam iron on the wrong side.
Stretch and mount the embroidery as explained on
page 9. Insert the mounted embroidery into the
frame, and assemble the frame according to the
manufacturer's instructions.

Backstitch and french knot details

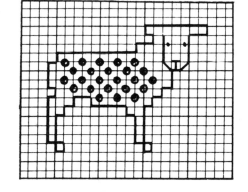
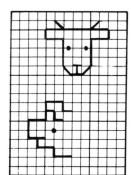

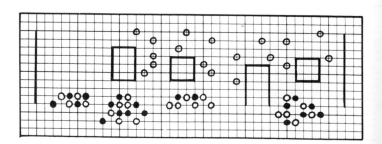

Farmhouse. The flowers in the farmhouse motif
are worked with two strands of cotton.
○ Yellow   ◖ Ecru
● Red   ⊕ Purple

FARMYARD ▶ SAMPLER		ANCHOR	DMC	MADEIRA
■	Grey	399	414	1801
+	Black	403	310	Black
T	Rich brown	358	433	2008
⊣	Pale brick	882	402	2307
▪	Pink	73	963	0608
⊓	Medium pink	1017	316	0809
∷	Yellow green	255	907	1410
S	Yellow	295	726	1019
⊓	Rust	349	301	2306
·	White	1	White	White
✕	Ecru	387	Ecru	1908
□	Brown	371	434	2009
⊢	Fawn	372	729	2209
⊓	Apple green	265	471	1501
⊠	Dark pink	1018	3726	0810
⊟	Rich green	257	905	1412
L	Blue	145	799	0910
Γ	Red	19	817	0211
⊐	Dark grey	400	317	1714
	Purple	110	209	0803

*Note: bks around the farmhouse walls, roof and windows, and
the pigs, sheep and cows in dark green* (*used for backstitch only);
bks the pig tails in pink, the sheep tails in ecru, the cow tails in black,
the hen legs and claws in fawn, and the stem of the climbing rose in
rich green. The french knots are shown on the detail charts only.*

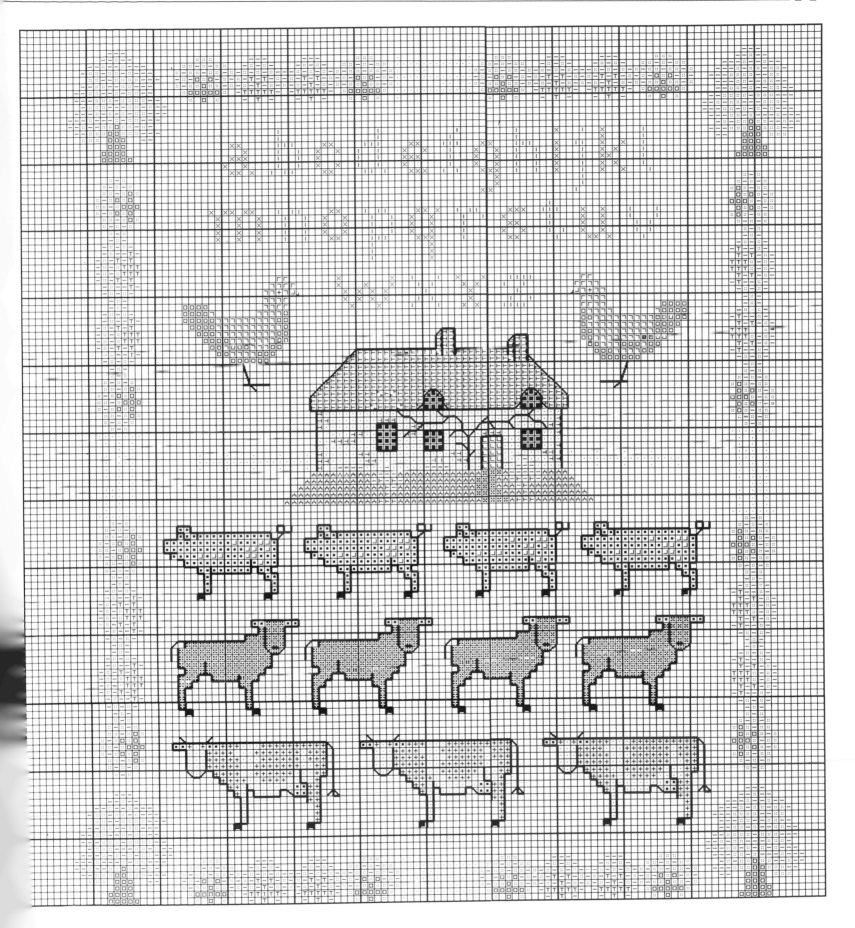

Home Sweet Home

The traditional text of this *Home Sweet Home* sample, embellished with a striking border, will help to make your house a home.

The sample uses a spectrum of sumptuous jewel shades – jade and emerald greens, pinks and purples – to complement the composition and create a vivid embroidery. The pattern of the deep border is richly resplendent, making the perfect frame for the traditional-style lettering.

HOME SWEET HOME

For the Home Sweet Home Sampler, with a design area measuring 23cm (9in) square, or 125 stitches each way, here in a frame measuring 36cm (14½in) square:

33cm (13in) square of white, 14-count
Aida fabric
Stranded embroidery cotton in the colours given
in the panel
No24 tapestry needle
Strong thread, for lacing across the back
Cardboard, for mounting, sufficient to fit into the
frame recess
Frame of your choice

•

THE EMBROIDERY

Prepare the fabric and stretch it in a frame as explained on page 5. Following the chart, start the embroidery at the centre of the design, using two strands of embroidery cotton in the needle. Work each stitch over one block of fabric in each direction, making sure that all the top crosses run in the same direction and each row is worked into the same holes as the top or bottom of the row before, so that you do not leave a space between the rows. For a simple sampler, the words 'Home Sweet Home' could be worked with just the inner border around the outside and for the finishing touch, you might add a row of stitching in dark magenta one square away from the inner border.

MAKING UP

Gently steam press the work on the wrong side and mount it as explained on page 9. Choose your own mount and frame from the large selection available in the shops or use one of the many framing services available to put the finishing touch to your work.

HOME SWEET HOME ▶		DMC	ANCHOR	MADEIRA
:	Light pink	776	73	0606
%	Dark pink	899	40	0609
>	Light mauve	3608	86	0709
+	Dark mauve	718	88	0707
v	Yellow	743	301	0113
x	Light green	320	215	1310
-	Medium green	367	216	1312
s	Dark green	319	217	1313

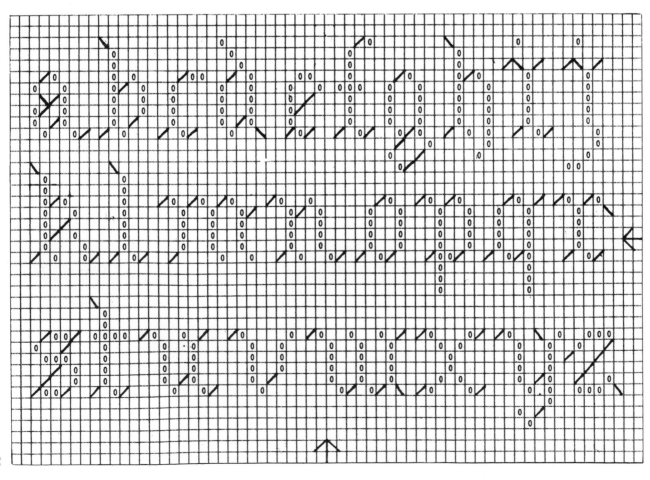

Alternative alphabet

Miniature Samplers

These little samplers make an
excellent introduction to cross stitch.
The projects are small, and quick to
complete, but provide the stitcher
with an attractive first embroidery.

MINIATURE SAMPLERS

YOU WILL NEED

For Love is Kind, with a design area measuring
14.5cm × 17.5cm (5¾in × 7in), or 81 stitches
by 97 stitches, here in a frame measuring
27cm × 30cm (10¾in × 12in):

*24cm × 28cm (9½in × 11in) of cream
14-count Aida fabric
Stranded embroidery cotton in the colours given
in the appropriate panel
No24 tapestry needle
Strong thread, for lacing across the back
Cardboard, for mounting, sufficient to fit into the
frame recess
Frame of your choice*

For Home Sweet Home, with a design area
measuring 17.5cm × 14cm (7in × 5½in), or
97 stitches by 77 stitches, here in a frame
measuring 30.5cm × 26cm (12¼in × 10½in):

*28cm × 24cm (11in × 9½in) of cream
14-count Aida fabric
Stranded embroidery cotton in the colours given
in the appropriate panel
No24 tapestry needle
Strong thread, for lacing across the back
Cardboard, for mounting, sufficient to fit into the
frame recess
Frame of your choice*

THE EMBROIDERY

Prepare the fabric and stretch it in a frame as explained on page 5. Following the appropriate chart, start the embroidery at the centre of the design, using two strands of embroidery cotton in the needle. Work each stitch over one block of fabric in each direction. Make sure that all the top crosses run in the same direction and that each row is worked into the same holes as the top or bottom of the row before so that you do not leave a space between the rows.

The bow and stalks on the *Love is Kind* sampler are worked in backstitch with two strands of green cotton, and the roses on the *Home Sweet Home* sampler are outlined with one strand of dark green cotton.

MAKING UP

Gently steam press the work on the wrong side and mount it as explained on page 9. The samplers could be framed as a matching pair or as two separate projects. The pine frames seen here complement the soft peach shades used for the embroideries, but these gentle shades could be exchanged for more vibrant colours to give a stronger feel to the designs.

Both samplers would look equally attractive stitched on an 11-count Aida fabric, which is particularly easy for a beginner to use. Remember that you may need extra stranded cotton for a design worked on an 11-count Aida because the stitches are bigger.

The *Love is Kind* sampler could be used as a small wedding sampler if the initials of the bride and groom were added, together with the date.

HOME SWEET HOME ◄		DMC	ANCHOR	MADEIRA
=	Pink	3688	68	0605
‹	Light peach	353	9	0304
+	Dark peach	352	10	0303
s	Light green	3052	844	1509
x	Dark green	319	218	1313
%	Brown	640	393	1905

LOVE IS KIND ►		DMC	ANCHOR	MADEIRA
c	Ecru	Ecru	926	Ecru
‹	Light peach	758	9575	0403
+	Dark peach	352	10	0303
x	Green	368	214	1310
%	Light brown	841	378	1911
=	Dark brown	829	906	2106

Traditional Sampler

This sampler would have looked perfectly at home hanging in a Victorian parlour around the turn of the century. A selection of traditional motifs of flowers and birds have been arranged to make this attractive design. Three of the motifs have been embroidered separately to make a delightful trio of pictures, or perhaps you would like to create a bellpull from the motifs, giving a truly Victorian flavour to your decor.

TRADITIONAL SAMPLER

YOU WILL NEED

For the Sampler and each of the small pictures derived from it, you will need the following, plus the individual requirements specified below:

Stranded embroidery cotton in the colours given in the appropriate panel
No24 tapestry needle
Strong thread, for lacing across the back
Cardboard, for mounting, sufficient to fit into the frame recess
Frame of your choice

For the Sampler, with a design area measuring 34cm × 25.5cm (13½in × 10¼in), or 183 stitches by 138 stitches, here in a frame measuring 40cm × 32.5cm (16in × 13in):

44cm × 35cm (17½in × 14in) of cream evenweave fabric, with 27 threads to 2.5cm (1in)

For the Rose picture, with a design area measuring 12cm × 13cm (4½in × 5in), or 64 stitches by 70 stitches, here in a frame measuring 18.5cm (7½in) square:

22cm × 23cm (8½in × 9in) of cream evenweave fabric, with 27 threads to 2.5cm (1in)

For the Cornflower picture, with a design area measuring 15cm × 11cm (6in × 4¼in), or 83 stitches by 59 stitches, here in a frame measuring 21cm × 16.5cm (8¼in × 6½in):

25cm × 21cm (10in × 8¼in) of cream evenweave fabric, with 27 threads to 2.5cm (1in)

CHART 1

For the Bird picture, with a design area measuring 11cm × 8cm (4¼in × 3in), or 59 stitches by 44 stitches, here in a frame measuring 16.5cm × 13.5cm (6½in × 5¼in):

21cm × 18cm (8¼in × 7¼in) of cream evenweave fabric, with 27 threads to 2.5cm (1in)

•

THE EMBROIDERY

For each design, prepare the linen and stretch in a frame as explained on page 5. Following the chart, start the embroidery at the centre of the design, using two strands of embroidery cotton in the needle. Embroider each stitch over two threads of fabric in each direction. Make sure that all the top crosses run in the same direction and each row is worked into the same holes as the row before so that you do not leave a space between the rows. Work the butterfly feelers with two strands of dark brown cotton in backstitch.

MAKING UP

Gently steam press the work on the wrong side and mount it as explained on page 9. To retain the traditional feel of the sampler, choose a simple wooden frame without a cardboard mount.

NOTE
The sampler has been divided into four charts, each showing a quarter.
The key and Charts 3 and 4 are on pages 124-125.

CHART 2

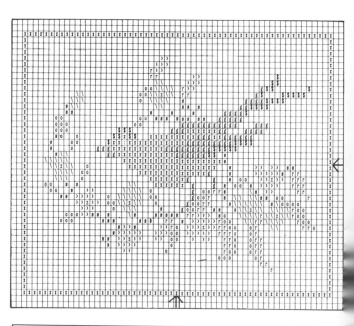

BIRD ▲		DMC	ANCHOR	MADEIRA
╲	Light mauve	341	117	0901
＜	Dark mauve	340	118	0902
g	Gold	834	874	2204
z	Dark yellow	725	298	0113
‡	Light blue	3325	976	1002
o	Light green	471	265	1502
r	Medium green	988	244	1402
s	Dark green	986	246	1404
x	Light brown	612	832	2002
$	Dark brown	370	856	2201

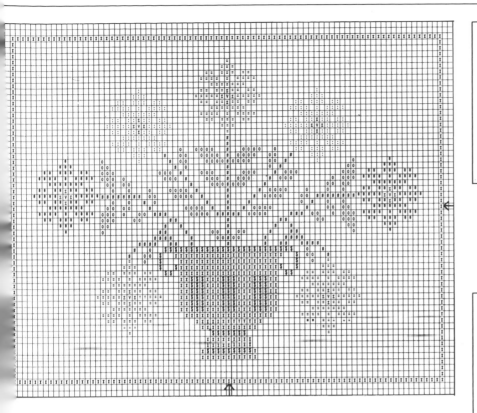

CORNFLOWER ◄		DMC	ANCHOR	MADEIRA
v	Light yellow	727	293	0110
z	Dark yellow	725	306	0108
‡	Light blue	3325	976	1002
:	Medium blue	334	977	1003
=	Dark blue	312	979	1005
o	Light green	471	265	1502
s	Dark green	986	246	1404
x	Light brown	612	832	2002
$	Dark brown	370	856	2201

ROSE ▼		DMC	ANCHOR	MADEIRA
%	Pale magenta	3609	85	0710
v	Light yellow	727	295	0111
z	Dark yellow	725	298	0113
o	Light green	471	265	1502
r	Medium green	988	244	1402
s	Dark green	986	246	1404
x	Light brown	612	832	2002
$	Dark brown	370	856	2201

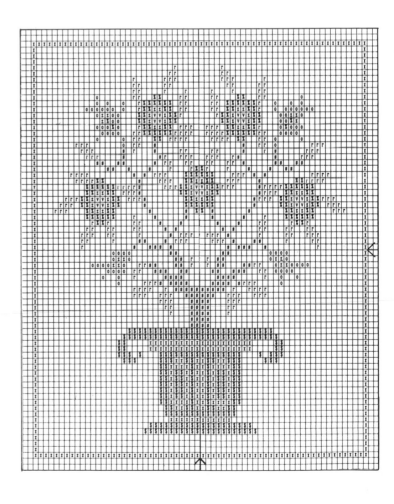

123

CHART 3

CHART 1	CHART 2
CHART 3	CHART 4

CHART 4

Butterfly Sampler

Decorated with butterflies,
this sampler reminds one of sunny
summer skies. The bright shades
of pink in the centre are echoed
in the floral border to continue
the theme. Stitch a feast for the
eye and revel in it!

BUTTERFLY SAMPLER

YOU WILL NEED

For the Butterfly Sampler, with a design area
measuring 22cm × 17.5cm (8½in × 7in), or
119 stitches by 97 stitches, here in a frame
measuring 34cm × 30cm (13½in × 12in):

*32cm × 27.5cm (12¾in × 11in) of
white, 14-count Aida fabric
Stranded embroidery cotton in the colours given
in the panel
No24 tapestry needle
Strong thread, for lacing across the back
Cardboard, for mounting, sufficient to fit into the
frame recess
Frame of your choice*

●

THE EMBROIDERY

Prepare the fabric and stretch it in a frame as
explained on page 5. Following the chart, start the
embroidery at the centre of the design, using two
strands of embroidery cotton in the needle. Work
each stitch over one block of fabric in each
direction. Make sure that all the top crosses run in
the same direction and each row is worked into the
same holes as the top or bottom of the row before so
that you do not leave a space between the rows.

Work the butterfly feelers in dark brown cotton,
backstitching over two blocks of fabric.

MAKING UP

Gently steam press the work on the wrong side and
mount it as explained on page 9. As this sampler has
a rather bright modern feel about it, one of the floral-
type frames might look attractive.

BUTTERFLIES ▶		DMC	ANCHOR	MADEIRA
%	Light pink	605	50	0613
+	Dark pink	602	63	0702
x	Yellow	3078	292	0102
c	Light blue	932	920	1602
s	Dark blue	311	148	1007
/	Light green	3052	844	1509
:	Dark green	3051	845	1508
=	Light brown	841	378	1911
⟩	Dark brown	640	393	1905

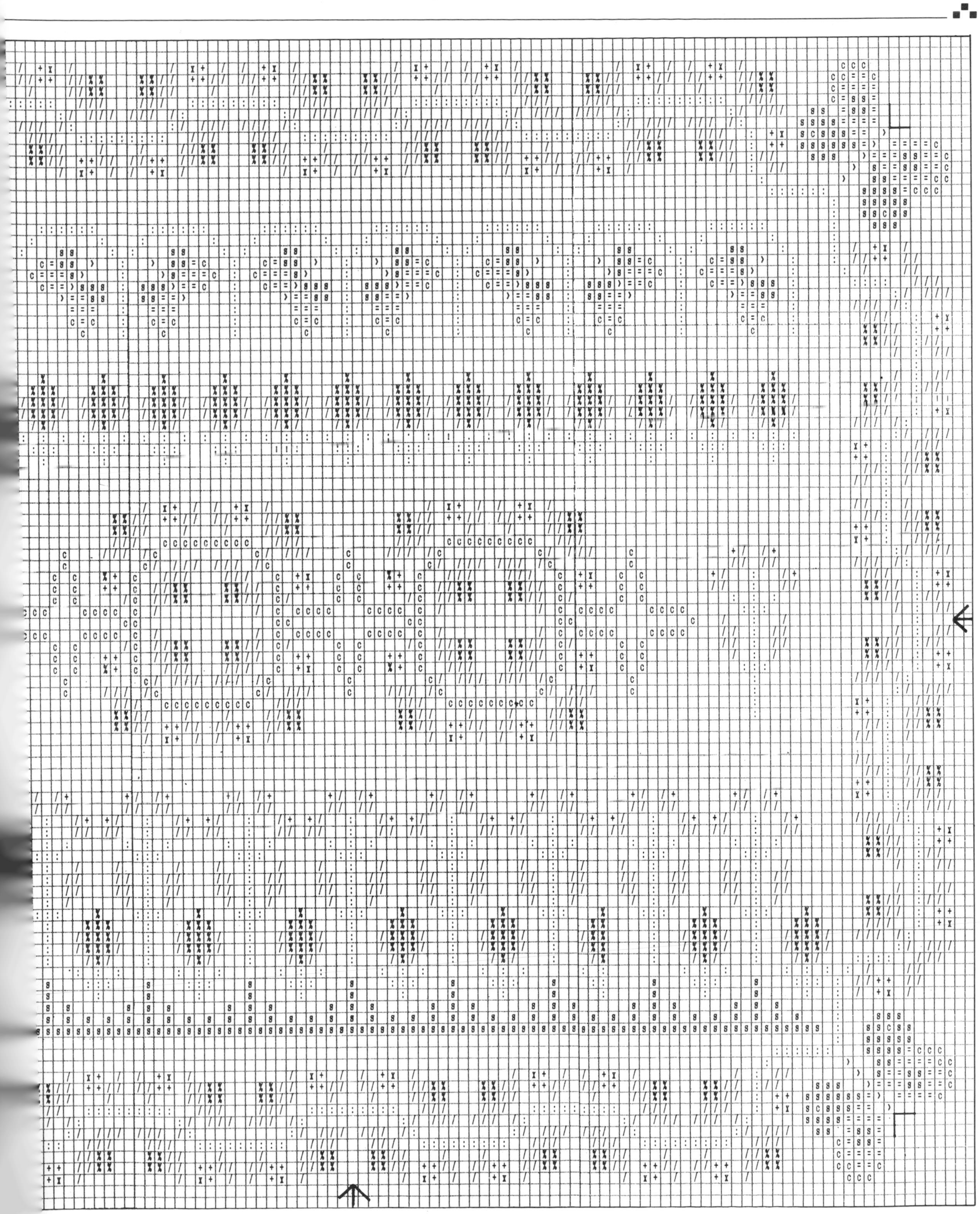

ALPHABETS

This chapter includes several beautiful cross stitch alphabets – including an amusing animal alphabet – which can be used to add a decorative and personal touch to a host of items, from greetings cards to framed samplers.

ANIMAL ALPHABET

YOU WILL NEED

For the Card, measuring 20cm × 15cm (8in × 6in), with an oval aperture measuring 15cm × 10cm (6in × 4in):

25cm × 20cm (10in × 8in) of white, 14-count Aida fabric
Stranded embroidery cotton in the colours given in the panel
No24 tapestry needle
Card, for suppliers see page 256

For the Framed Initial, here in a frame measuring 15cm × 11.5cm (6in × 4½in), with an aperture measuring 13cm × 10cm (5¼in × 4in):

20cm × 15cm (8in × 8in) of white, 14-count Aida fabric
Stranded embroidery cotton in the colours given in the panel
No24 tapestry needle
Frame of your choice

NOTE: the letters vary in size, and the embroidery for both the card and the picture can be worked on virtually any count of evenweave fabric.

For the Bib, measuring 18.5cm × 15cm (7⅜in × 6in):

Stranded embroidery cotton in the colours given in the panel
No24 tapestry needle
Evenweave bib, for suppliers see page 256

To embroider initials on purchased (non-evenweave) clothes:

Stranded embroidery cotton in the colours given in the panel
No24 tapestry needle
Waste canvas, with 14 threads per 2.5cm (1in), a piece 5cm (2in) larger each way than the dimensions of the finished embroidered initial
Fine tweezers
Water Spray
Basting cotton and needle
Chosen item of clothing

THE CARD

Prepare the fabric, marking the centre with horizontal and vertical lines of basting stitches. Mount it in a hoop as explained on page 5. Start the stitching at the centre, using two strands of cotton in the needle, if using 14-count Aida (see stitching details). Take each stitch over one block of fabric in each direction, making sure that all the top crosses run in the same direction and that each row is worked into the same holes as the top or bottom of the row before, so that you do not leave a space between rows.

MAKING UP

Gently steam press the embroidery on the wrong side and trim it to measure 12mm (½in) larger each way than the aperture. Centre your embroidery behind the opening and secure it in place with double-sided tape. Press the card firmly together.

THE FRAMED INITIAL

The embroidery is worked in the same way as for the card. Gently steam press the finished embroidery on the wrong side; mount it (see page 9), and set it in a frame of your choice.

THE BIB

Mark the centre of the bib with horizontal and vertical lines of basting stitches, and embroider your chosen initial (see individual stitching details), using two strands of embroidery cotton in the needle and taking each stitch over one block of the fabric.

When you have finished, remove the basting stitches and gently steam press the bib on the wrong side.

USING WASTE CANVAS

Position the blue threads of the canvas horizontally or vertically with the weave of the garment. Pin and then baste the canvas in place and remove the pins. Each pair of canvas threads is treated as one thread, so the cross stitch is worked over one pair of threads in each direction. Start stitching in the centre, which you can mark on the canvas with a vertical and horizontal line of basting stitches. Begin the embroidery by fastening the cotton with your first stitches, and finish by threading the cotton through a few stitches at the back of the work. Make sure that you start and finish firmly, so that the stitches do not pull out during washing.

When the cross stitching is complete, trim the

canvas to within 12mm (½in) of the embroidery. Dampen the embroidery on the right side with warm water and leave for a few minutes until the threads soften. Using tweezers, pull the canvas threads out one at a time so that you do not damage your embroidery.

Press the embroidery by placing it right side down on a towel and pressing with a hot iron and damp cloth.

ALPHABET STITCHING DETAILS

All letters are worked using three strands of stranded cotton for 11-count fabric, two for 14-count fabric and one for 18- or 22-count fabric.

All outlining is in backstitch, using one strand of dark grey unless stated otherwise. Additional stitching details are as follows:

The letter B
Embroider the bee's wings in backstitch with one strand of dark grey.

The letter C
Embroider the whiskers in backstitch with two strands of black cotton.

The letters E and J
Embroider the water in backstitch with two strands of dark blue.

The letter I
Embroider the feelers in backstitch, using two strands of black cotton.

The letter L
Embroider the feelers in backstitch, using two strands of black cotton.

The letter R
Embroider the whiskers in backstitch with one strand of dark grey cotton.

The letter S
Embroider the whiskers in straight stitch with one strand of black cotton.

The letter U
Embroider the tufts of hair in backstitch with two strands of yellow cotton.

The letter V
Embroider the vipers' tongue in backstitch, using two strands of black cotton.

The letter W
Embroider the water in backstitch with two strands of pale blue.

ANIMAL ALPHABET		DMC	ANCHOR	MADEIRA
C	Light gold	676	887	2208
V	Dark gold	729	890	2209
/	Light brown	437	362	2011
=	Medium brown	435	(363)	2009
Z	Dark brown	434	365	2008
X	Moss green	471	265	(1501)
S	Light jade green	563	208	1207
W	Dark jade green	562	210	(1206)
r	Red	349	(46)	0212
.	Yellow	743	301	0109
e	Light blue	800	128	1014
n	Dark blue	799	130	1012
+	Light grey	318	235	1802
>	Medium grey	414	399	1801
-	Pink	604	60	(0614)
a	Mauve	340	118	0902
*	Black	Black	403	Black
0	White	White	1	White
	Dark grey*	3799	(236)	(1713)

Note: numbers in brackets indicate the nearest colour match; for bks outline use dark grey (*used for bks only).*

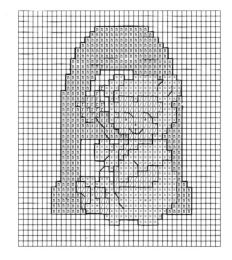

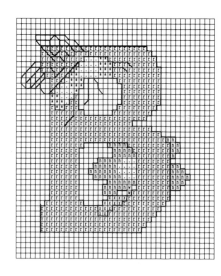

Turn to page 136 for charts for the remaining letters.

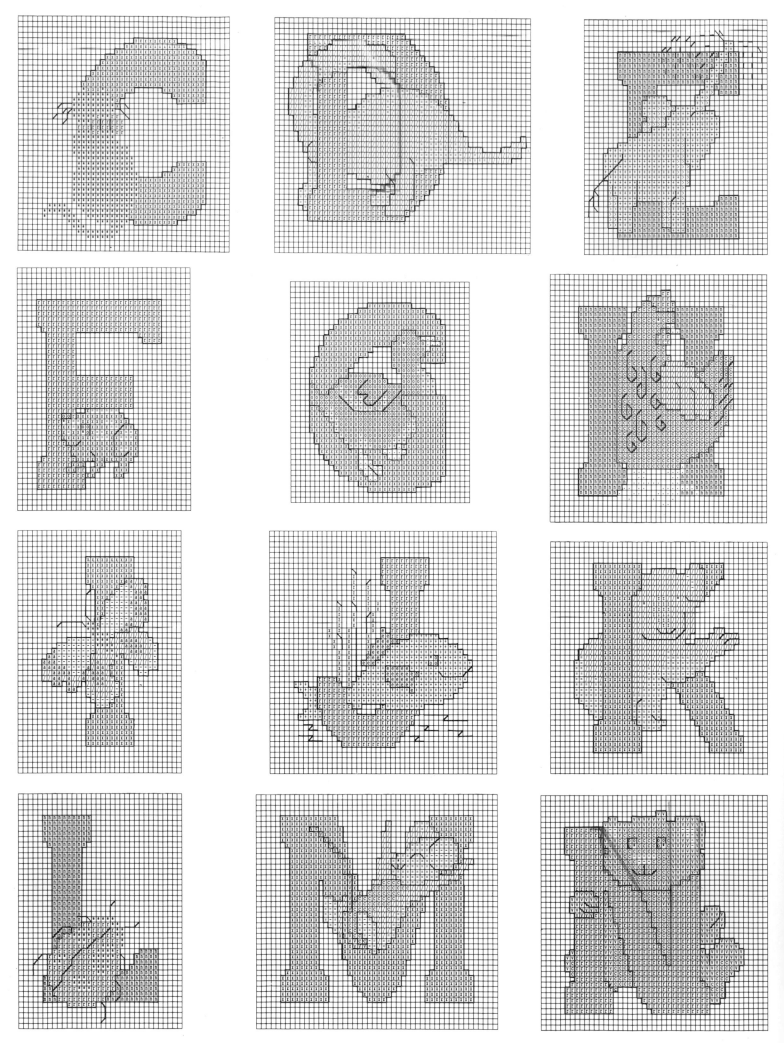

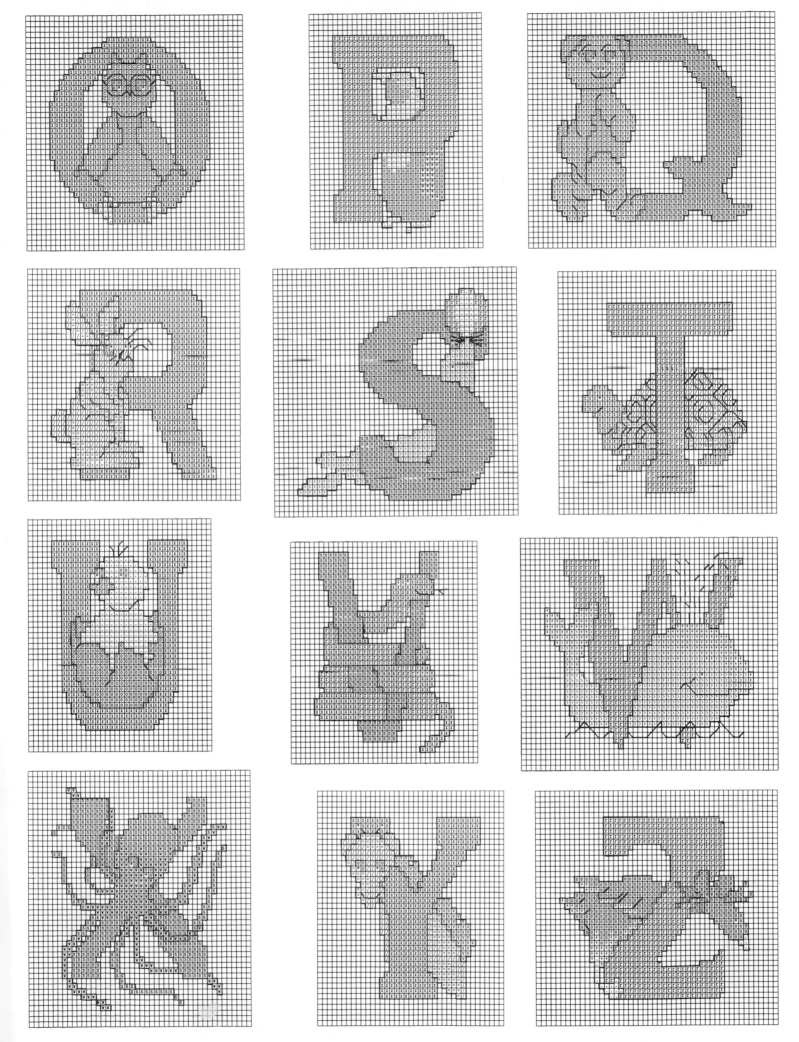

Wreath Alphabet

Charming wreaths of flowers or fruits make a highly versatile alphabet. The paperweight or the box with a rosebud wreath would grace any lounge, while the fruit garland might encircle covers for homemade jams and preserves.

WREATH ALPHABET

YOU WILL NEED

For the Paperweight, measuring 6.5cm (2½in) in diameter:

10cm (4in) square of white, 18-count Aida fabric
Stranded embroidery cotton in the colours given in the panel
No 26 tapestry needle

For the Porcelain box, with a lid measuring 9cm (3½in) in diameter:

13cm (5¼in) square of cream, 14-count Aida fabric
Stranded embroidery cotton in the colours given in the panel
No 24 tapestry needle

For each Jam-pot Cover, measuring 15.5cm (6¼in) in diameter, with a central circle of 18-count Aida fabric, measuring 6.5cm (2½in) in diameter:

Ready-prepared cover, for suppliers, see page 256
70cm (28in) of matching ribbon, 6mm (¼in) wide
Stranded embroidery cotton in the colours given in the panel
No 26 tapestry needle

For the Card, measuring 13cm × 16.5cm (5¼in × 6½in), with an aperture measuring 9.5cm (3¾in):

15cm (6in) square of white, 14-count Aida fabric
Stranded embroidery cotton in the colours given in the panel
No 24 tapestry needle
Purchased card, for suppliers, see page 256

For the Pot-pourri Pillow, measuring 25cm (10in) square, excluding the lace edging:

27.5cm (11in) square of white Schonfells fabric, with a 12-count centre, 9.5cm (3¾in) in diameter
27.5cm (11in) square of white cotton fabric
2.4m (2¾yd) of lace edging, 4cm (1½in) wide
Polyester filling
Pot-pourri sachet
Stranded embroidery cotton in the colours given in the panel
No 24 tapestry needle
White sewing cotton and needle

THE PAPERWEIGHT

Prepare the fabric and mark the centre with horizontal and vertical lines of basting stitches. Mount it in a hoop as explained on page 5. Start the stitching at the centre, using one strand of embroidery cotton in the needle. Work each stitch over one block of fabric in each direction. Make sure that all the top crosses run in the same direction and that the top or bottom of each row is worked into the same holes as the row before, so that you do not leave a space between the rows.

Outline the flowers with one strand of dark green cotton.

MAKING UP

Centre the finished embroidery on the cream backing paper provided with the paperweight, using the basting lines as a guide. Trim the fabric carefully to the size of the paper. Remove basting stitches and place the embroidery and paper face downwards in the recess at the bottom of the paperweight; secure both with the adhesive felt backing disc.

THE BOX

Prepare the fabric and mark the centre with horizontal and vertical lines of basting stitches. Mount it in a hoop as explained on page 5. Start the stitching at the centre, using two strands of cotton in the needle. Work each stitch over one block of fabric in each direction. Make sure that all the top crosses run in the same direction and that the top or bottom of each row is worked into the same holes as the row before so that you do not leave a space between the rows. Outline flowers and embroider stalks in backstitch, using one strand of dark green cotton.

Gently steam press the embroidery on the wrong side. Use the basting stitches as a guide to centre the design, removing them when you have trimmed the fabric. Follow the manufacturer's instructions for assembling the lid.

JAM-POT COVERS

For each cover, prepare the fabric and mark the centre with horizontal and vertical lines of basting stitches. Mount it in a hoop as explained on page 5. Start the stitching at the centre, using one strand of embroidery cotton in the needle. Take each stitch over one block of fabric in each direction. Make sure that all the top crosses run in the same direction and that the top or bottom of each row is worked into the same holes as the row before so that you do not leave a space between the rows.

Outline the flowers and berries and work the stalks in backstitch, using one strand of dark green cotton in the needle. The seeds on the strawberries are worked with cream french knots (see page 8). Tie the finished cover to your jar with a matching length of coloured ribbon.

THE CARD

Prepare the fabric and mark the centre with horizontal and vertical lines of basting stitches. Mount it in a hoop as explained on page 5. Start the stitching at the centre, using two strands of embroidery cotton in the needle. Work each stitch over one block of fabric in each direction. Make sure that all the top crosses run in the same direction and that each row is worked into the same holes as the top or bottom of the row before, so that you do not leave a space between the rows.

Outline the flowers and embroider the stalks in backstitch, using one strand of dark green cotton in the needle.

MAKING UP

Gently steam press the embroidery on the wrong side and trim to measure 12mm (½in) larger each way than the aperture. Centre your embroidery behind the opening and secure it in place with double-sided tape. Press the card firmly together.

POT-POURRI PILLOW

Prepare the fabric and mark the centre with horizontal and vertical lines of basting stitches. Mount the fabric in a frame or hoop as explained on page 5. Start the stitching at the centre, using three strands of embroidery cotton in the needle. Work each stitch over one block of fabric in each direction. Make sure that all the top crosses run in the same direction and that each row is worked into the same holes as the top or bottom of the row before, so that you do not leave a space between the rows.

Work the stalks in backstitch, with one strand of dark green cotton in the needle.

MAKING UP

Gently steam press the work on the wrong side. Join the edges of the lace together with a small french seam and run a gathering thread along the edge of the lace. Pull the gathers up to fit around the edge of the pillow and, with right sides together and the lace lying on the fabric with the decorative edge facing inwards, baste the lace to the edge of the embroidery, just inside the 12mm (½in) seam allowance. Spread the gathers evenly, allowing the extra fullness at the corners, and machine stitch in place. Place the backing fabric on top, right sides together; baste, and then machine stitch in place, taking a 12mm (½in) seam allowance and leaving a 20cm (8in) opening along one side. Remove basting stitches; trim across the corners, and turn the pillow cover right side out. Fill with loose polyester wadding and the pot-pourri sachet; slipstitch the opening.

WREATH ALPHABET		DMC	ANCHOR	MADEIRA
–	Light mauve	208	111	0804
S	Dark mauve	550	101	0714
Z	Pink	3689	66	0606
r	Crimson	3608	86	0709
X	Light moss green	3052	844	1509
=	Dark moss green	3051	845	1508
0	Bright green	3348	264	1409
.	Cream	746	275	0101
e	Yellow	743	301	0113
V	Light blue	800	128	0909
+	Dark blue	799	130	0910
n	Light red	349	12	0212
C	Dark red	304	47	0513
/	Brown	640	393	1905

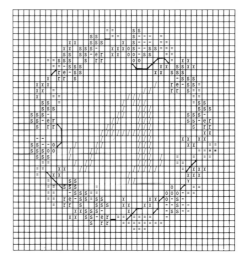

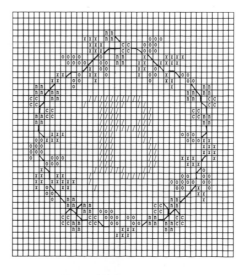

Turn to page 144 for charts for the remaining letters.

141

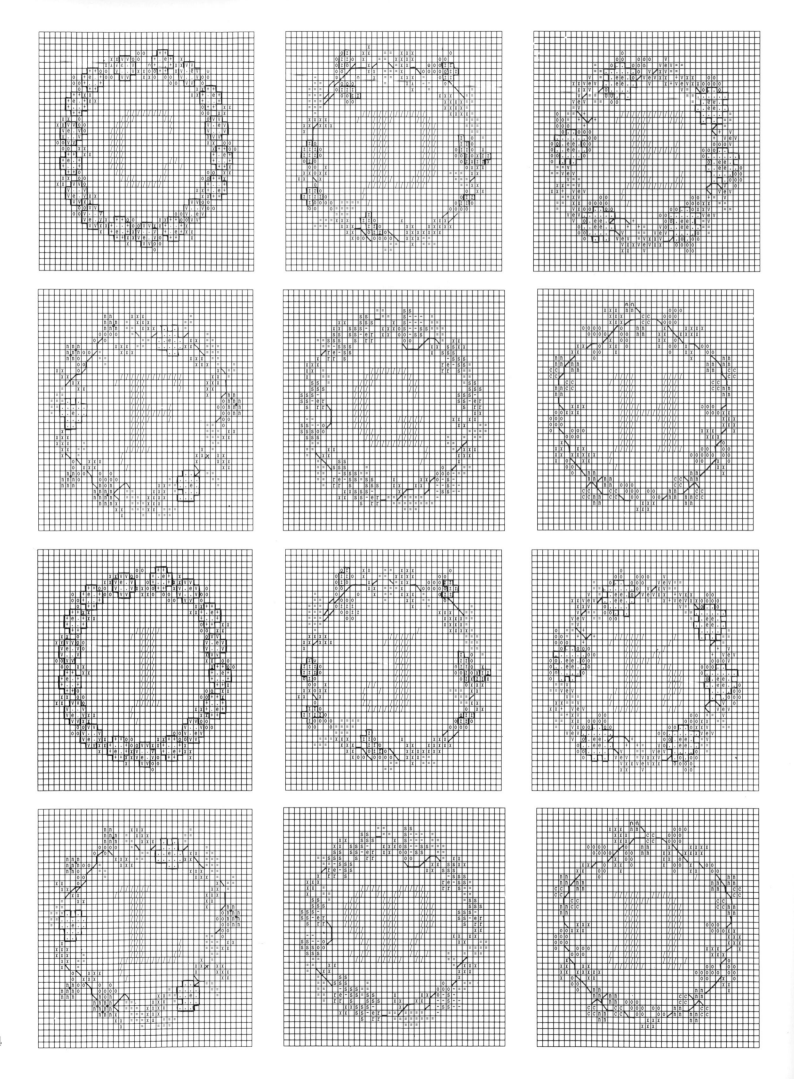

145

Traditional Alphabet Sampler

Letters and patterns such as these adorned the parlours of Victorian ladies. This simplified version is designed to bring a traditional air to a room setting.

TRADITIONAL ALPHABET SAMPLER

YOU WILL NEED

For the Traditional Alphabet Sampler, with a design area measuring 24cm × 17cm (9½in × 6¾in) or 137 stitches by 96 stitches, here in a frame measuring 34cm × 27cm (13½in × 10¾in):

35cm × 28cm (14¼ × 11½in) of beige, 28-count Quaker cloth
Stranded embroidery cotton in the colours given in the panel
No 24 tapestry needle
Strong thread, for lacing across the back
Cardboard for mounting, sufficient to fit into frame recess
Frame of your choice

•

THE EMBROIDERY

Prepare the fabric, and baste horizontal and vertical centre lines (see page 5). Stretch the fabric in a frame, as explained on page 5. Following the chart, start the embroidery at the centre of the design, using two strands of embroidery cotton in the needle. Work each stitch over two threads of fabric in each direction. Make sure that all the top crosses run in the same direction and that each row is worked into the same holes as the top or bottom of the row before, so that you do not leave a space between the rows.

MAKING UP

Gently steam press the work on the wrong side and mount it as explained on page 9. To retain the traditional feel of the sampler, choose a simple wooden frame without a cardboard mount.

TRADITIONAL ALPHABET ▶		DMC	ANCHOR	MADEIRA
V	Gold	834	874	2204
X	Dark blue	930	922	(1712)
=	Light blue	931	921	(1711)
S	Dark brown	3790	905	2003
r	Light brown	640	393	1905
0	Dark green	3362	263	1601
−	Light green	3052	844	1509
e	Dark peach	922	337	0310
+	Light peach	402	347	2307

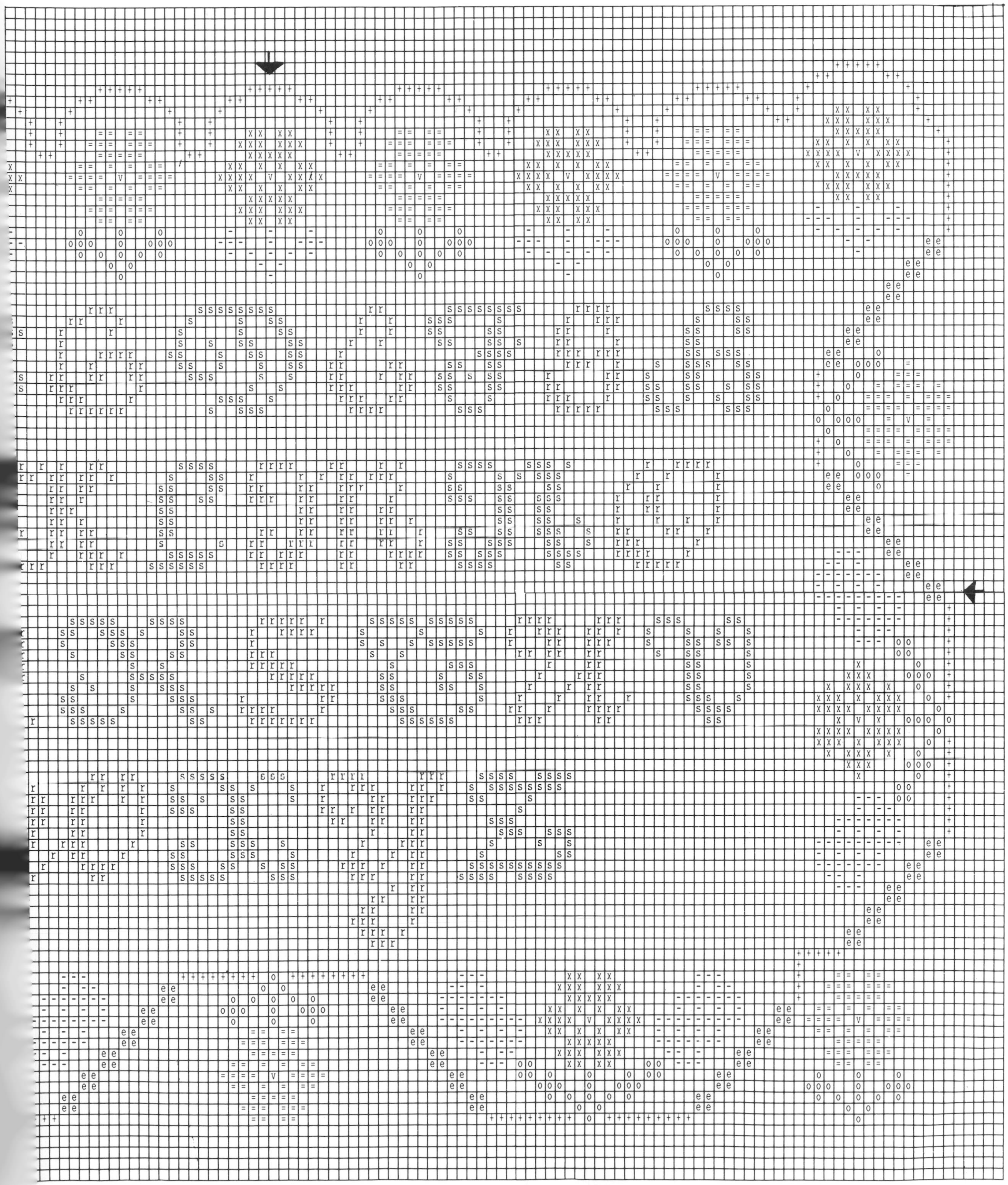

Modern Alphabet Sampler

This alphabet, with its subtle combination of greens, greys and mauves, would fit easily into most modern colour schemes. Choose a mount to enhance your own particular decor.

MODERN ALPHABET SAMPLER

YOU WILL NEED

For the Modern Alphabet Sampler, with a design area measuring 18.5cm × 25.5cm (7¼in × 10¼in), or 101 stitches by 155 stitches, here in a frame measuring 32cm × 39cm (12¾in × 15½in):

30cm × 37cm (12in × 14¾in) of white, 14-count Aida fabric
Stranded embroidery cotton in the colours given in the panel
No 24 tapestry needle
Strong thread, for lacing across the back
Cardboard for mounting, sufficient to fit into the frame recess
Frame of your choice

●

THE EMBROIDERY

Prepare the fabric, marking the centre with horizontal and vertical lines of basting stitches, and stretch it in a frame as explained on page 5. Following the chart, start the embroidery at the centre of the design, using two strands of embroidery cotton in the needle. Work each stitch over one block of fabric in each direction. Make sure that all the top crosses run in the same direction and that each row is worked into the same holes as the top or bottom of the row before, so that you do not leave a space between the rows.

MAKING UP

Gently steam press the finished embroidery on the wrong side and mount it as explained on page 9. Choose a suitably modern frame to display your sampler.

MODERN ALPHABET ▶		DMC	ANCHOR	MADEIRA
−	Dark mauve	208	111	0804
S	Light mauve	211	342	0801
V	Dark grey	415	398	1803
=	Light grey	762	234	1804
0	Dark green	367	216	1312
X	Light green	368	214	1310

Note: bks lines in one strand of dark green.

TOP

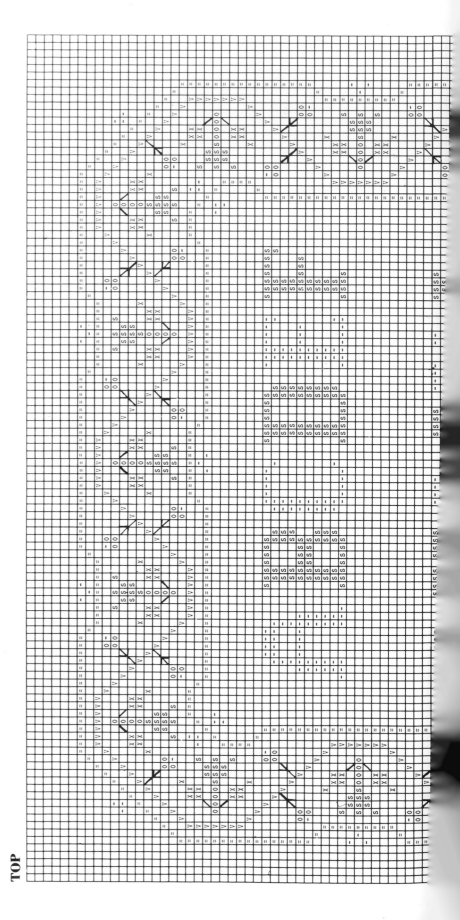

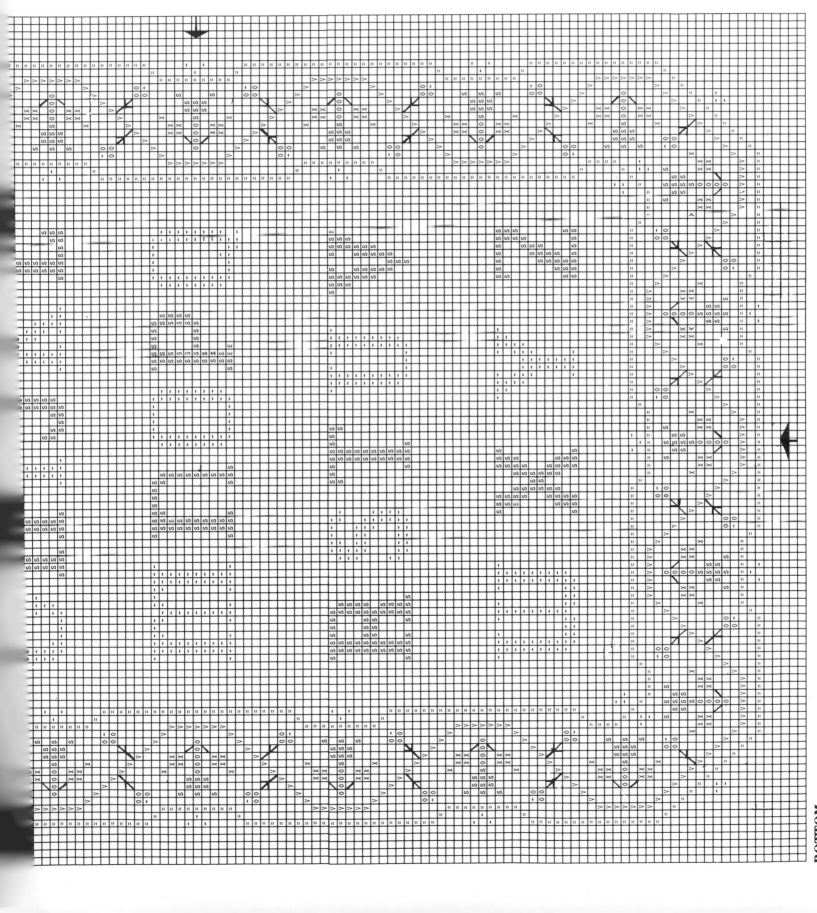

Lower Case
Alphabet

Sometimes you may want to stitch a
full name or a message, rather than
just an initial. Here is a choice of
cross stitch alphabets designed
to go with the more elaborate
initials of the previous pages.

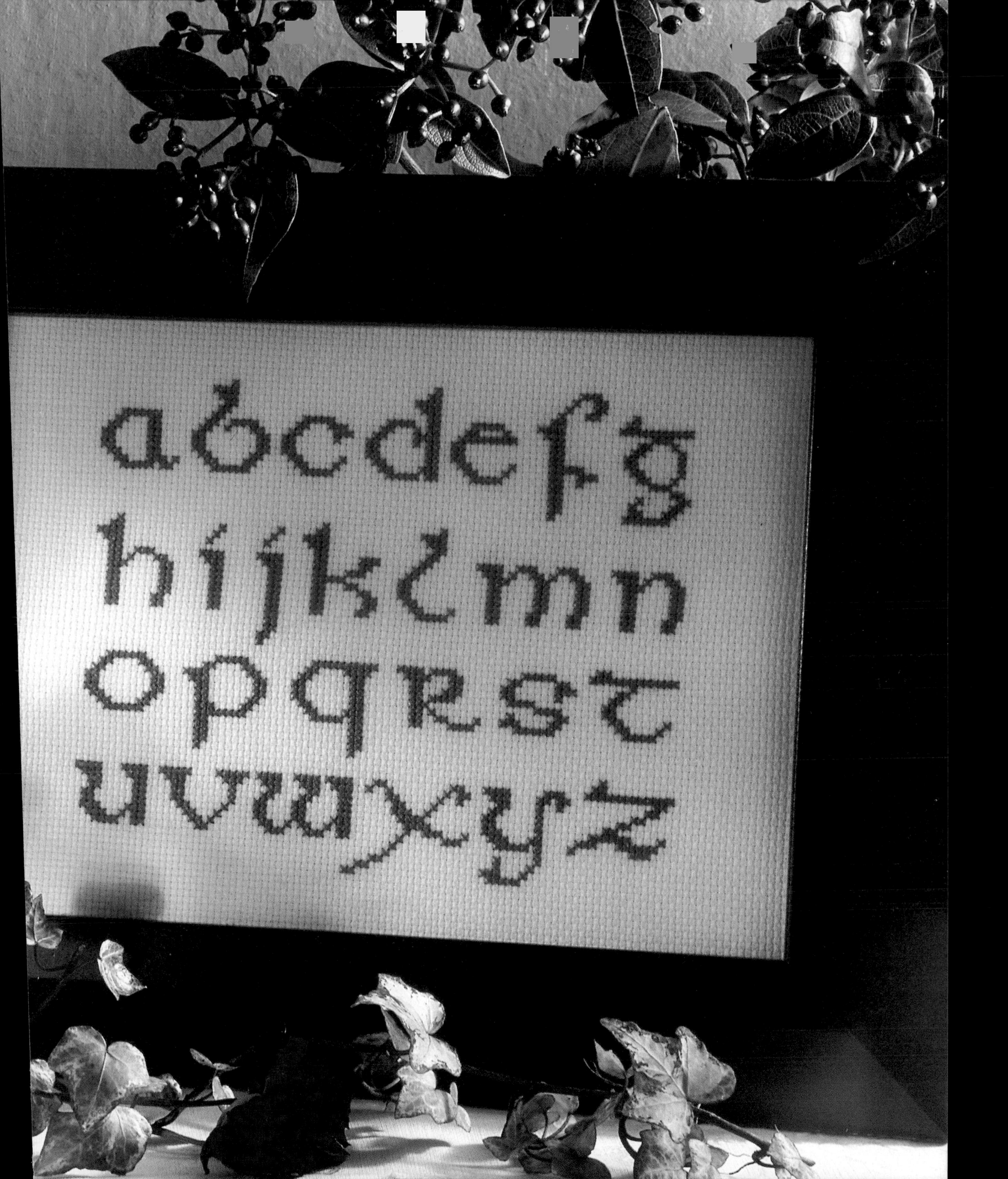
abcdefg
hijklmn
opqrst
uvwxyz

LOWER CASE ALPHABET

To use this alphabet, it is necessary first to work out the spacing on graph paper. This alphabet is designed to be used with any of the capital/initial alphabets given in this book, and can be stitched in whichever colour is appropriate for your particular project.

The lower case cross stitch alphabets given here would be ideal for many purposes – adding a name to the centre of a sampler, for example. There are other cases, however, where the cross stitch lettering would be too large and cumbersome; for example, you might wish to make a Valentine's Day card with a verse of poetry, starting with an elaborate cross stitch initial from the Wreath alphabet. In this case, it would be better to 'write' the words in backstitch lettering, perhaps in an italic effect.

To do this, take a sheet of graph paper and a pencil and first draw out the initial, as shown here. Next, write out the rest of the verse, using your chosen handwriting. Go over the writing again, remembering that each backstitch must be indicated by a line either running from corner to corner of a square or horizontally (see the backstitching of the Animal alphabet).

When you are making your backstitch chart, remember that the scale will be the same as that of the charted initial. If you are not sure about the stitched size, make a small sample of the lettering on your chosen fabric before stitching the main project.

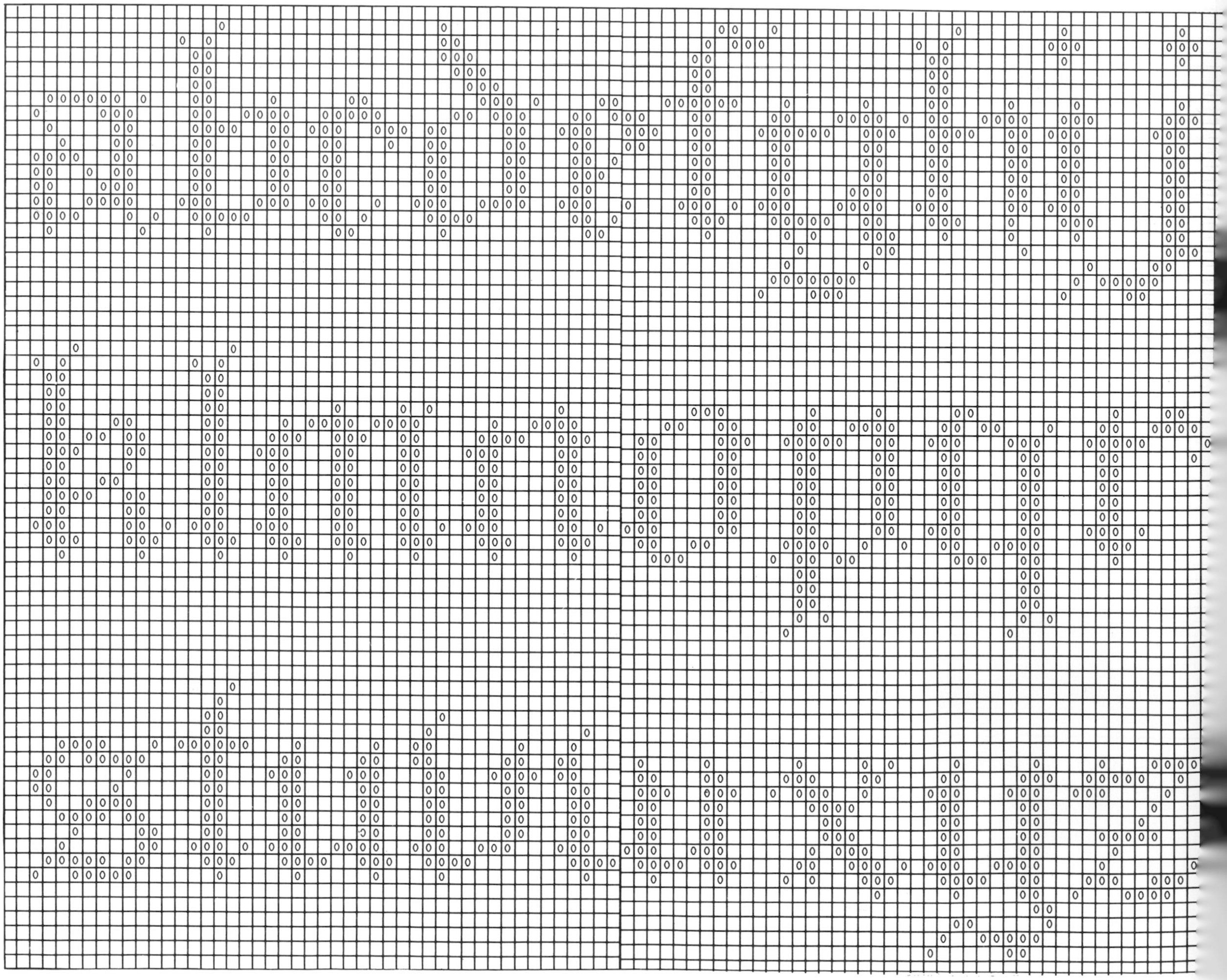

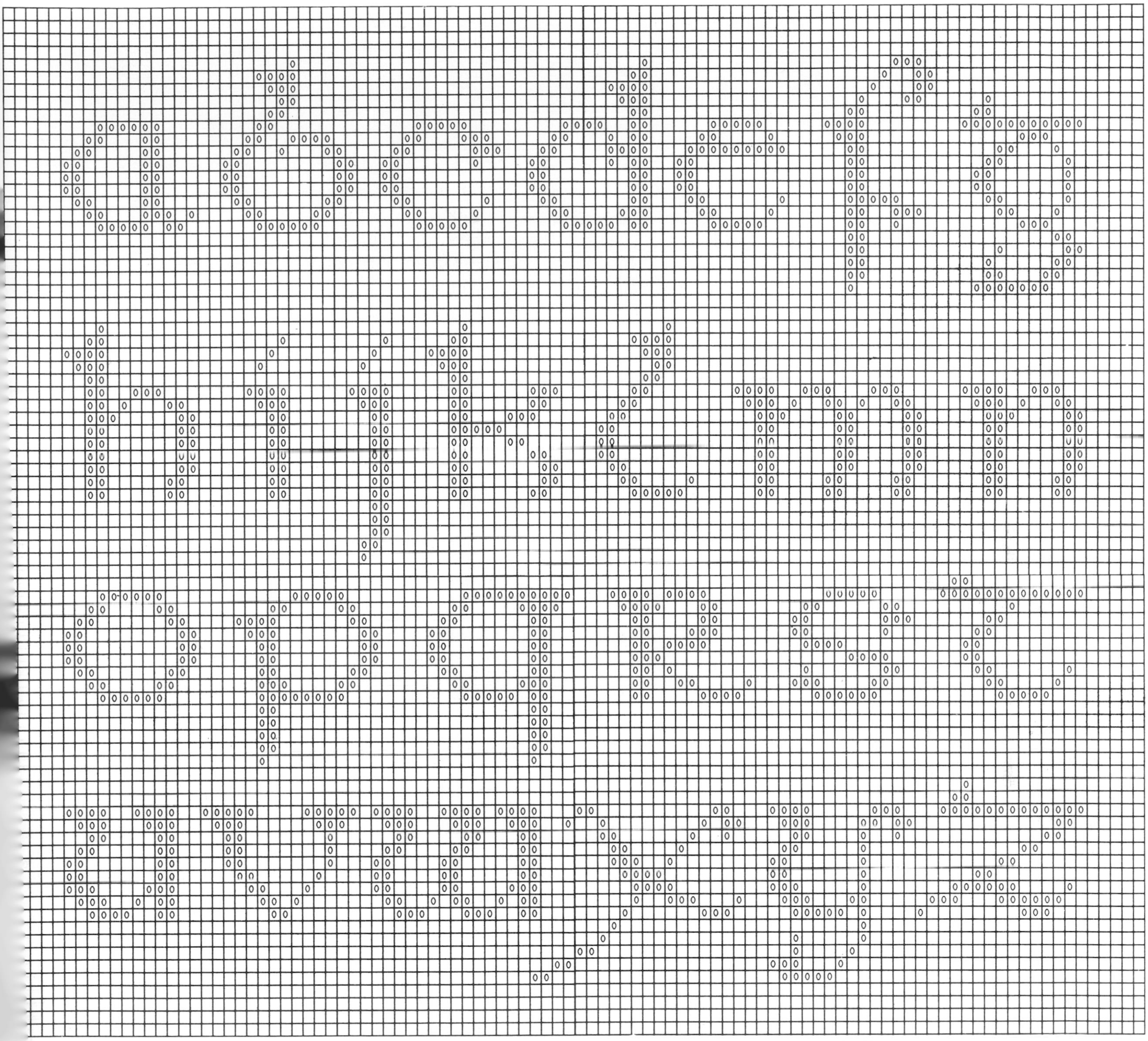

QUICK AND EASY PROJECTS

These simple cross stitch projects are ideal for those with little free time. Now, when you get a spare hour or two, you can stitch yourself a photo frame, a greetings card or even a set of coasters.

GARDEN BIRDS CARDS

YOU WILL NEED

For each Card, with a square aperture measuring
6.8cm (2⅝in) each way:

12.5cm (5in) square of cream, 11-count Aida fabric
Stranded embroidery cotton in the colours given in
the appropriate panel
No24 tapestry needle
Card, as specified above (for suppliers, see page 256)

NOTE: *one skein of each colour on the combined
list is sufficient for all five designs. The fabric
quantity quoted above includes an allowance of
6.5cm (2½in) each way, for framing; if you are
making more than one card, allow a 10cm (4in)
square for each, plus a 5cm (2in) margin around the
total area.*

•

THE EMBROIDERY

Prepare the fabric as described on page 5; find
the centre by folding the fabric in half and then in
half again, and lightly pressing the folded corner, or
by marking the horizontal and vertical centre lines
with basting stitches in a light-coloured thread. If
you are stitching several designs at once, separate
the card areas (10cm/4in square) with lines of
basting stitches, and mark the centre of each area,
but do not cut them apart until you have finished
the embroidery. Mount the prepared fabric in a
hoop or frame.

Following the chart, complete all cross stitching,
using two strands of thread in the needle. Be
careful not to take dark threads across the back of
the work in such a way that they show through on the
right side. Finish with the backstitching, again using
two strands of thread. Stitch each bird's eye,
indicated by a black dot on the chart, with a single
french knot (see page 8).

GARDEN BIRDS (all five)		ANCHOR	DMC	MADEIRA
✖	Black	403	Black	Black
•	White	1	White	White
V	Medium grey	399	318	1802
••	Light grey	398	415	1803
⊡	Light beige	852	3033	2109
+	Yellow beige	373	422	2103
2	Light brown	310	780	2009
⊞	Dark brown	360	898	2005
■	Dark red	20	498	513
▫	Red	19	347	510
●	Deep pink	39	309	507
○	Light pink	33	3706	409
H	Deep orange	332	946	0207
↓	Light orange	316	740	204
⠢	Yellow green	278	472	1414
◇	Olive	280	733	1611
⊓	Medium green	257	905	1412
✕	Dark green	268	937	1504
=	Blue	979	312	1010

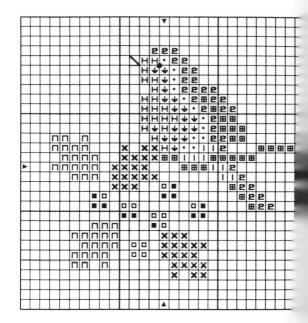

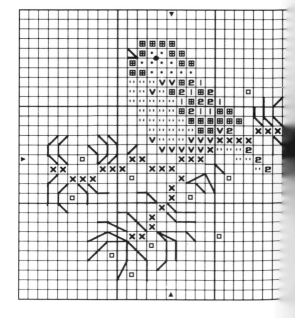

TREE SPARROW ▶		ANCHOR	DMC	MADEIRA	
•	White	1	White	White	*Note: bks the fir cone*
	Black*	403	Black	Black	*outlines in dark green*
⊞	Dark brown	360	898	2005	*and the beak in black**
2	Light brown	310	780	2009	*(*used for backstitching*
⊡	Light beige	852	3033	2109	*and french knot only);*
••	Light grey	398	415	1803	*make the eye with one*
V	Medium grey	399	318	1802	*black french knot.*
✕	Dark green	268	937	1504	
▫	Red	19	347	510	

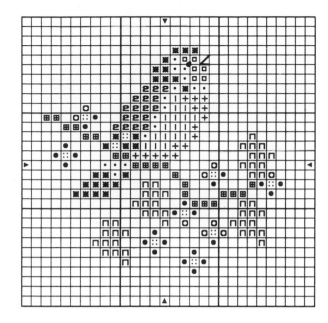

GOLDFINCH ◄		ANCHOR	DMC	MADEIRA
✳	Black	403	Black	Black
•	White	1	White	White
⊞	Dark brown	360	898	2005
2	Light brown	310	780	2009
I	Light beige	852	3033	2109
+	Yellow beige	373	422	2103
▢	Red	19	347	510
⊓	Medium green	257	905	1412
∷	Yellow green	278	472	1414
●	Deep pink	39	309	507
○	Light pink	33	3706	409

Note: bks the beak in black, and make the eye with a black french knot.

ROBIN ◄		ANCHOR	DMC	MADEIRA
	Black*	403	Black	Black
•	White	1	White	White
I	Light beige	852	3033	2109
2	Light brown	310	780	2009
⊞	Deep brown	360	898	2005
⊓	Medium green	257	905	1412
✕	Dark green	268	937	1504
▢	Red	19	347	510
■	Dark red	20	498	513
↓	Light orange	316	740	204
H	Deep orange	332	946	0207

Note: bks the beak in black (*used for backstitching and french knot only), and make the eye with a black french knot.*

BRAMBLING ▲		ANCHOR	DMC	MADEIRA
•	White	1	White	White
✳	Black	403	Black	Black
⊞	Dark brown	360	898	2005
2	Light brown	310	780	2009
I	Light beige	852	3033	2109
+	Yellow beige	373	422	2103
↓	Light orange	316	740	0204
H	Deep orange	332	946	0207
O	Light pink	33	3706	409
●	Deep pink	39	309	507
V	Medium grey	399	318	1802
⊓	Medium green	257	905	1412

Note: bks the beak in black, and make the eye with a black french knot.

BLUE TIT ◄		ANCHOR	DMC	MADEIRA
•	White	1	White	White
✳	Black	403	Black	Black
=	Blue	979	312	1010
⊞	Dark brown	360	898	2005
⊓	Medium green	257	905	1412
✕	Dark green	268	937	1504
▢	Red	19	347	510
■	Dark red	20	498	513
∷	Yellow green	278	472	1414
◇	Olive	280	733	1611

Note: backstitch the cherry stems in dark green, and the head and beak in black; make the eye with a black french knot.

161

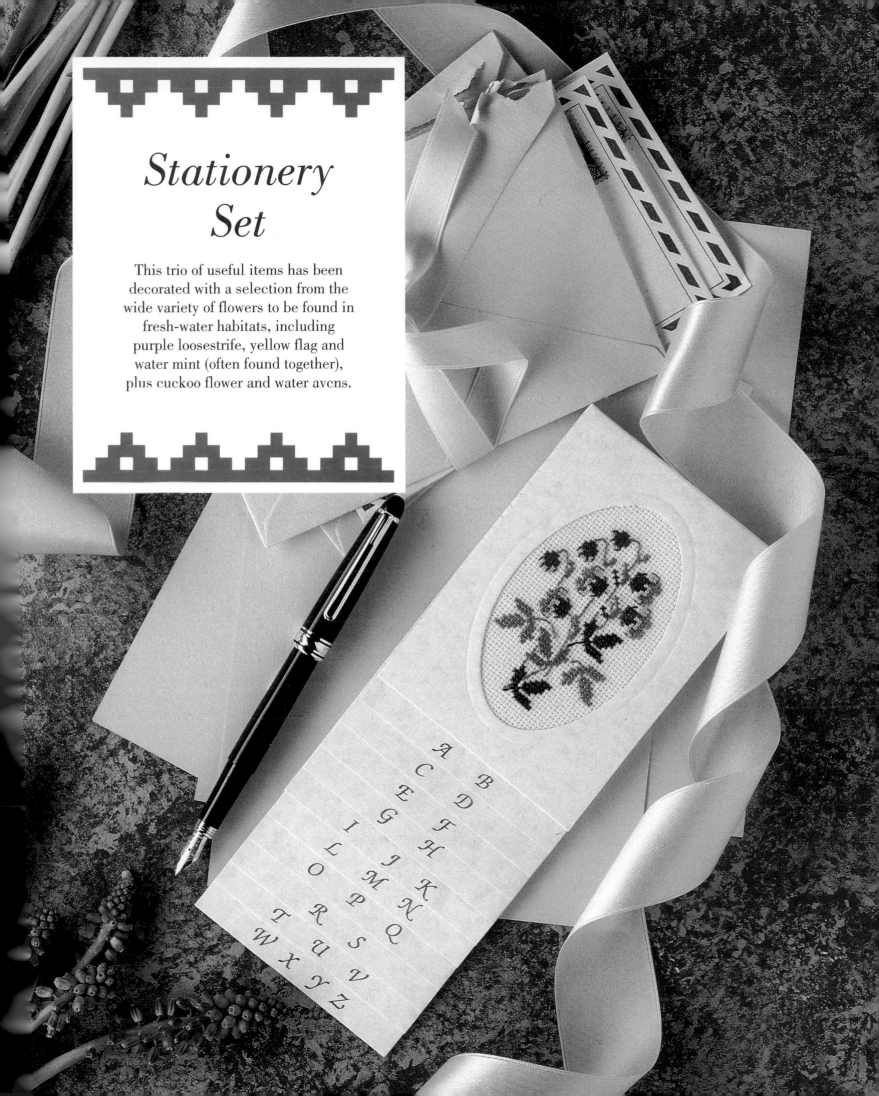

Stationery Set

This trio of useful items has been decorated with a selection from the wide variety of flowers to be found in fresh-water habitats, including purple loosestrife, yellow flag and water mint (often found together), plus cuckoo flower and water avens.

STATIONERY SET

YOU WILL NEED

For the Address Book, measuring 20cm × 15cm (8in × 6in):

*53cm × 30.5cm (21in × 12in) of cream,
18-count Aida fabric
47cm × 16.5cm (18½in × 6½in) of white interfacing
Stranded embroidery cotton in the colours given in
the appropriate panel
No26 tapestry needle
An address book of your choice*

For the Stamp Book, measuring 9.5cm × 7.5cm (3³⁄₄in × 3in):

*21cm × 10cm (8¼in × 4in) of white,
14-count perforated paper
21cm × 10cm (8¼in × 4in) of stiff white paper,
for lining
Stranded embroidery cotton in the colours given in
the appropriate panel
No24 tapestry needle
51cm (20in) of green ribbon, 6mm (¼in) wide*

For the Telephone Index Pad, measuring 22.5cm × 8.5cm (8³⁄₄in × 3½in), with an oval aperture measuring 8.5cm × 5.5cm (3½in × 2in):

*13cm × 11cm (5in × 4½in) of cream,
18-count Aida fabric
Stranded embroidery cotton in the colours given in
the appropriate panel
No26 tapestry needle
A blank telephone index pad, prepared for
embroiderers (for suppliers, see page 256)*

•

THE EMBROIDERY

For the address book, fold the Aida in half, giving you a working area of 26.5cm × 30.5cm (10½in × 12in). With the fold on the left, measure in 12mm (½in) from the fold and baste from top to bottom. Measure a further 15cm (6in) across and baste another, parallel line. Baste two horizontal lines 20cm (8in) apart and equidistant from the top and bottom edges of your working area. This will leave a 20cm × 15cm (8in × 6in) rectangle for the front cover. Place the design towards the bottom left-hand side of the rectangle, leaving a 1.5cm (⅝in) margin on both sides. Add two lines of basting stitches to mark the

position of these margins. Begin at the bottom left of the chart. Use two strands of cotton for cross stitches, and two strands for backstitching, except for the insect, where only one strand is used. Steam press on the wrong side when complete.

For the stamp book, using a soft pencil, draw a line dividing the paper into two areas, each measuring 10.5cm x 10cm (4¼in x 4in). This pencil line will be the fold of the stamp book. Position your embroidery so that the left-hand cross stitch frame is approximately 7mm (¼in) to the right of your pencil line. Working the frame first, stitch your embroidery, using three strands of cotton for the cross stitches and two strands of cotton for the backstitching.

For the telephone index pad, find the centre of your piece of Aida, and start your embroidery from the centre of the design. Use two strands of cotton for the cross stitches and two strands for the backstitching. Steam press on the wrong side when complete.

MAKING UP THE ITEMS

For the address book cover, centre the interfacing on the back of the Aida fabric. Fold the Aida to form a narrow hem along all the edges, enclosing the interfacing, and machine stitch into position. Centre the address book on the wrong side of the fabric and fold the extra width over the free side edges of the front and back covers. Seam along the edges at the top and bottom to form pockets at the front and back.

For the stamp book cover, fold the perforated paper along the pencil line to form the cover for your stamp book. Fold your stiff lining paper in two and carefully stick it in position inside your already folded perforated paper. Fold the ribbon along the spine of the stamp book and make a bow on the front. Books of stamps will slip inside and you can keep them in place by slotting them through the ribbon.

The telephone index pad comes with all you need to mount the embroidery and assemble the pad.

WATER AVENS TELEPHONE INDEX PAD ▶				
(Geum rivale)		DMC	ANCHOR	MADEIRA
6	Lemon	727	293	0110
▽	Dark green	3362	263	1601
⊟	Bluish green	3363	261	1602
·	Green	3347	266	1408
S	Dull purple	315	1019	0810
T	Purplish pink	3688	66	0605
U	Pink	3689	49	0607
	Dull pink*	3687	68	0604
	Dusky pink*	223	895	0812

Note: bks stalk of bluish-green leaf in bluish green; the flower sepals in dull purple; the petals in dull pink; the stalks of the dark green leaves in green; the stalks of the dark green leaves in dark green, and the flower stems in dusky pink* (*used for backstitch only).*

PURPLE LOOSESTRIFE, YELLOW FLAG & WATER MINT ADDRESS BOOK
(Lythrum salicaria, Iris pseudacorus & Menta aquatica)

		DMC	ANCHOR	MADEIRA
⊟	White	White	1	White
▯	Dark brown	3031	905	2003
4	Yellow	725	306	0108
5	Lemon	726	262	0109
▽	Dark green	3345	268	1406
△	Green	3346	262	1407
+	Light green	3347	266	1408
·	Pale green	3348	265	1409
↖	Very dark green	3362	263	1601
→	Bluish green	3363	261	1602
↑	Light blue green	3364	260	1603
X	Yellow green	472	264	1414
⊓	Ginger brown	435	365	2010
L	Deep lilac	208	111	0804
Z	Lilac	210	108	0802
C	Pale lilac	211	342	0801
●	Deep pink	3607	87	0708
H	Pink	3608	86	0709
■	Pale pink	3609	85	0710
	Grey*	413	401	1713
	Dusky pink*	223	895	0812

Note: bks the fly's wings and legs, and the flower centres of the loosestrife in grey; the stems of the water mint in dusky pink* (*used for backstitch only); the fly's body, the lighter leaves of the loosestrife and the leaf veins of the water mint in pale green; the stamens of the loosestrife in deep pink; the leaf veins of the darker loosestrife leaves in light green, and the detail on the iris flower in ginger brown.*

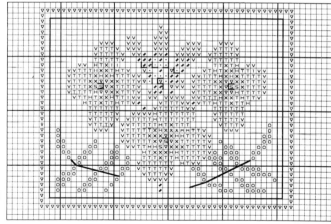

CUCKOO FLOWER STAMP BOOK ▲
(Cardamine pratensis)

		DMC	ANCHOR	MADEIRA
5	Yellow	725	306	0108
▽	Green	470	267	1502
O	Bluish green	3363	261	1602
·	Pale green	472	264	1414
⁄	Light green	471	266	1501
X	Cream	746	275	0101
V	Purplish pink	3608	86	0709
H	Greyish pink	316	969	0809
T	Pink	3609	85	0710
	Dark grey*	413	401	1713

Note: bks the leaf stalks in bluish green, the border in green; and the flower centres and detail at the base of the buds in dark grey (*used for backstitch only).*

Set of Coasters

These attractive coasters would make ideal gifts for dog lovers. They can be used for drinks glasses or for small items on a dressing table, and make presents which are both decorative and functional.

SET OF COASTERS

YOU WILL NEED

For each Coaster, with a working area of 7.5cm (3in) in diameter and a design area of 5cm (2in), or German Shepherd 38 stitches by 38 stitches, Spaniel 33 stitches by 35 stitches, and Rough Collie 35 stitches by 39 stitches:

15cm (6in) square of cream, 18-count Aida fabric
Stranded embroidery cotton in the colours given
in the appropriate panel
No26 tapestry needle
15cm (6in) square of iron-on interfacing
Glass coaster (for suppliers, see page 256)

•

THE EMBROIDERY

Prepare the edges of the fabric and mark the central vertical and horizontal design lines with basting stitches. Stretch the fabric in a frame, following the instructions on page 5. Start the embroidery at the centre of the design, using two strands of thread in the needle. Gently steam press the finished embroidery on the wrong side.

MAKING UP

Remove the basting stitches and iron the interfacing to the wrong side of the embroidery. Lay the embroidery face-down on a flat surface and, using the paper template provided with the coaster, draw around the design, ensuring that it is central. Check that the template line is correct by laying the coaster over the top, and then carefully cut out the circle. Place the embroidery face-down in the recess on the base of the coaster, and place the paper template on top of the reverse side of the embroidery. Peel the backing from the protective base and carefully place it over the back of the coaster, ensuring that the embroidery and paper template remain in position.

SPANIEL ▼		DMC	ANCHOR	MADEIRA
•	Dark brown	938	380	2005
⋈	Dark tan	433	358	2008
•|•	Medium tan	434	310	2009
S	Light tan	435	365	2010
◁	Very light tan	436	363	2011
→	Dark beige	437	362	2012
V	Medium beige	738	361	2013
+	Light beige	739	366	2014
■	Black	310	403	Black
▬	Grey	646	8581	1812
◤	Very light grey	3072	847	1805

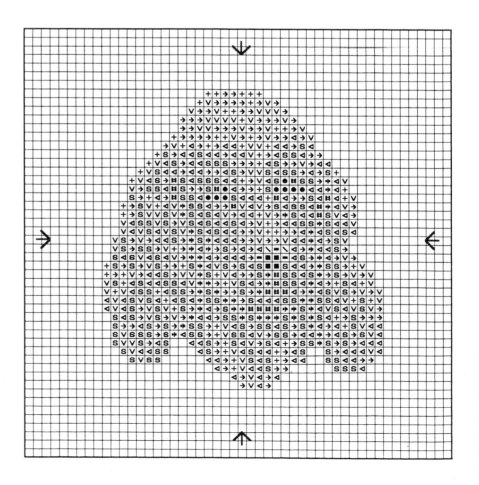

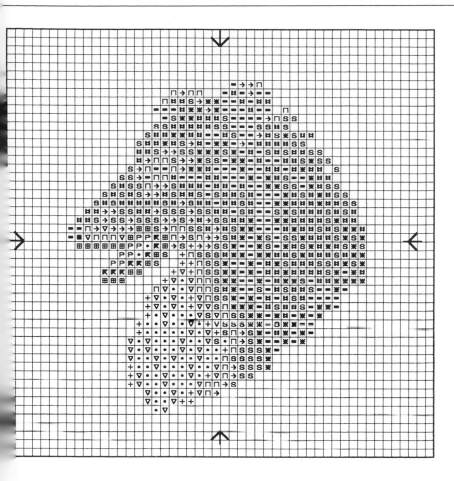

ROUGH COLLIE ◄	DMC	ANCHOR	MADEIRA
• White	White	2	White
P Dark pink	221	896	0811
▬ Very dark brown	938	380	2005
✳ Dark brown	801	359	2007
⋈ Dark tan	433	358	2008
S Medium tan	435	365	2010
→ Light tan	436	363	2011
⊓ Dark honey	738	361	2013
+ Honey	739	366	2014
▽ Light grey	3072	847	1805
⊞ Medium grey	647	8581	1813
◩ Dark grey	844	401	1810
■ Black	310	403	Black

GERMAN SHEPHERD ►	DMC	ANCHOR	MADEIRA
╲ Beige pink	950	4146	2309
+ Light pink	224	894	0813
P Dark pink	223	895	0812
✳ Dark brown	801	359	2007
⊓ Very light tan	738	361	2013
→ Light tan	437	362	2012
▨ Medium tan	436	363	2011
S Dark tan	435	365	2010
◉ Very dark tan	434	310	2009
▽ Light grey	648	900	1814
• White	White	2	White
⊞ Dark grey	646	8581	1812
◩ Very dark grey	844	401	1810
■ Black	310	403	Black

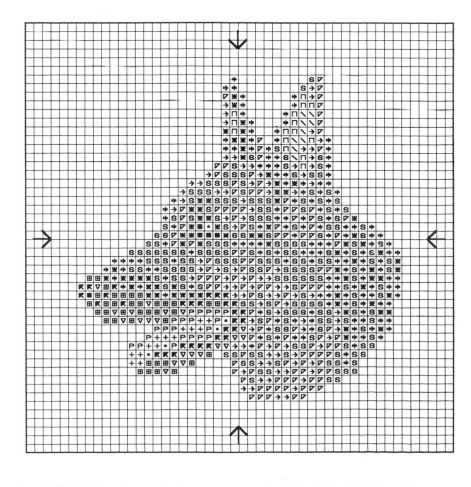

Clown Faces

Even the plainest of children's clothes can be turned into something special with these clown faces and (optional) numerals. With the use of the waste canvas technique, these small designs can be added to clothes made from non-evenweave fabrics, and you can also make a card to accompany your gift.

CLOWN FACES

To embroider either of these decorations on your chosen item of children's clothing:

*16cm × 14cm (6¹/₄in × 5¹/₂in) of waste canvas
(for suppliers see page 256), with 14 double
threads per 2.5cm (1in)
Stranded embroidery cotton in the colours given in
the appropriate panel
No24 tapestry needle
Fine tweezers
Water spray*

For each matching card, measuring 20cm × 15cm
(8in × 6in):

*24cm × 19cm (9¹/₂in × 7¹/₂in) of white,
18-count Aida fabric
A piece of iron-on interfacing, approximately
15cm (6in) square (optional)
Stranded embroidery cotton in the colours given in*

*the appropriate panel
No26 tapestry needle
Double-sided adhesive tape
Card mount (for suppliers see page 256)*

•

THE EMBROIDERY

To ensure that your finished embroidery lies straight on the garment, align the blue threads of the canvas horizontally or vertically, either with the weave of the fabric or with the seams of the garment. Pin and baste the canvas centrally over the design area and remove the pins (see page 7).

Treat each pair of canvas threads as a single thread, and stitch the design as you would on any other evenweave fabric. Start stitching at the top of the design and work downwards, using two strands for the cross stitch, and one for the backstitch. When you have finished, remove the waste canvas threads, following the instructions on page 7.

If you choose to sew your design onto fabric which is dry-cleanable only, the canvas threads can be softened by rubbing them together (taking care

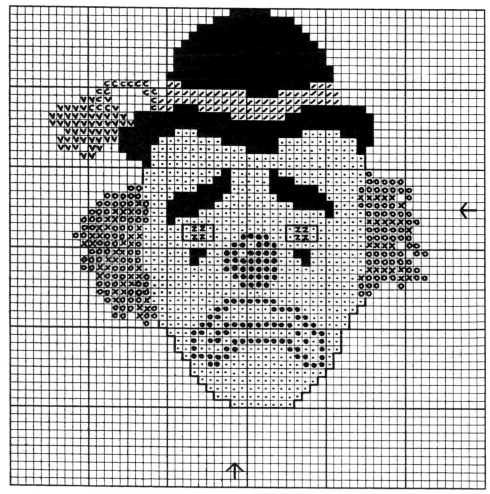

SAD CLOWN

not to damage the embroidery). It should then be possible to remove the threads one by one, without having to use water.

THE CARDS

Both cards are stitched in the same way and on the same type of fabric. Prepare the fabric, marking the centre lines of each design with basting stitches, and mount it in a small hoop, following the instructions on page 5. Referring to the appropriate chart, complete the cross stitching, using two strands in the needle, and finish with the backstitching, using one strand in the needle. Steam press on the wrong side if required.

It is not strictly necessary to use iron-on interfacing, but it helps to avoid wrinkles. If you are using interfacing, place it on the back of the embroidery; use a pencil to mark the basting/registration points on the interfacing and outer edge of the embroidery. Remove the basting stitches and iron the interfacing in place, aligning marks.

Trim the embroidery to measure about 12mm (¹/₂in) larger than the cut-out window, and then, making sure that the motif is placed in the middle by measuring an equal distance at each side of the marks, position the embroidery behind the window. Use double-sided tape to fix the embroidery into the card, then press the backing down firmly.

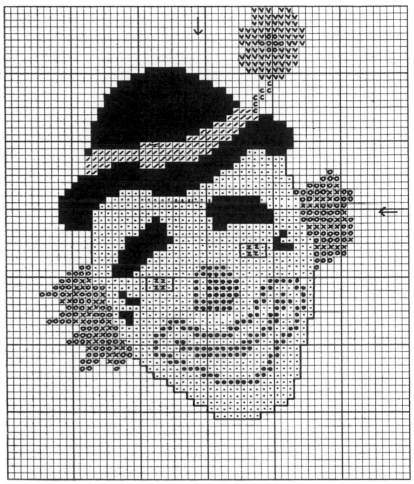

SMILING CLOWN

CLOWN FACES	DMC	ANCHOR	MADEIRA
■ Black	310	403	Black
◪ Very dark lavender	208	110	0804
⊙ Medium tangerine orange	741	304	0201
☒ Medium burnt orange	946	332	0207
· White	White	2	White
● Bright Christmas red	666	46	0210
▾ Dark lemon yellow	444	291	0108
⊏ Chartreuse green	703	238	1307
☒ Medium delft blue	799	130	0910

Note: bks with black.

For a birthday card, you might like to stitch the appropriate number as given in the chart below.

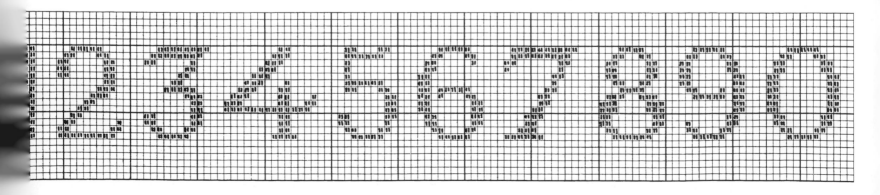

Pierrot Frames

These enchanting photograph frames will make a cheerful and amusing addition to your home, whether displayed individually or as a pair. Either of the two designs would make a lovely present for an adult or a child.

PIERROT FRAMES

YOU WILL NEED

For each Pierrot frame measuring 30.5cm × 23cm
(12in × 9in):

38cm × 30.5cm (15in × 12in) of 20-count,
silver fleck Bellana fabric
Stranded embroidery cotton in the colours given in
the appropriate panel
No26 tapestry needle
30.5cm × 23cm (12in × 9in) of white
mounting board
Scalpel, craft knife or scissors
Masking tape
Craft adhesive
9cm (3¹/₂in) of white ribbon, 6mm (¹/₄in) wide,
for a hanging loop
Thin white card to back the frame

THE EMBROIDERY

For each frame, prepare the fabric and stretch it in a
hoop or frame (see page 5). Embroider the design in
the relevant bottom corner of the fabric, 6.5cm
(2¹/₂in) in from the raw edges of the fabric at the side
and bottom. Using one strand of thread in the needle

PIERROT WITH A FLOWER ▼	DMC	ANCHOR	MADEIRA
■ Black	310	403	Black
· White	White	2	White
╱ Pale grey	415	398	1803
Z Medium shell grey	452	906	1807
● Light red	350	11	0213
∴ Light lavender	211	342	0801
V Dark lavender	209	105	0803
X Very dark lavender	208	110	0804
‖ Medium steel grey	317	400	1714
│ Light shell grey	453	375	1806
Rich red*	817	9046	0211

Note: bks the eyebrows and eyelid with black, use medium shell
grey for the face, and rich red (*used for bks only) for the lips.*

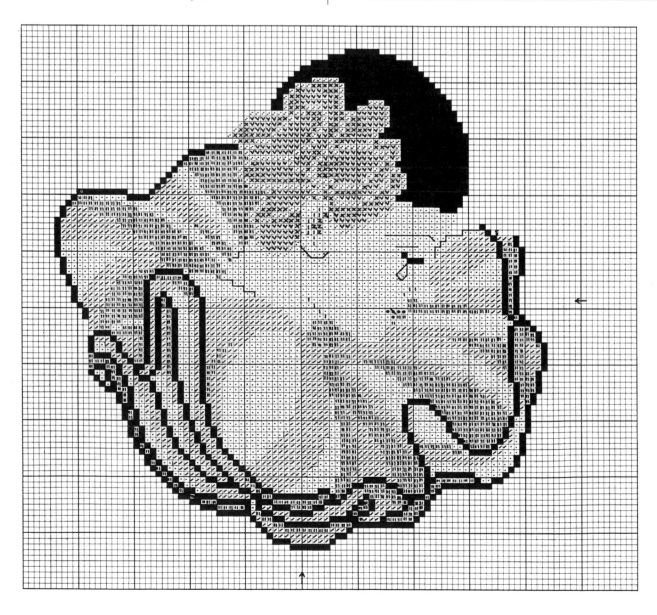

throughout, complete the cross stitching first, and finish off with the backstitching. Leaving the basting stitches in at this stage, as guidelines, gently press the finished embroidery on the wrong side with a steam iron.

MAKING THE FRAME

Carefully cut out a window from the mounting board: the windows of the frames shown here measure 9.5cm (3³/₄in) square, and are positioned 5cm (2in) in from the top and side edges of the mounting board, diagonally opposite the embroidery. You can, however, cut the window to whatever size or shape you wish.

Place your embroidery face down on a firm, flat surface and, using the basting stitches as a guide, position the mounting board on top of it. Next, mark the cut-out on the fabric with a soft pencil. Remove the basting stitches and, using a sharp pair of scissors, make a small nick in the centre of the marked cut-out in the fabric, and cut diagonally from the centre up to each marked corner. Place the mounting board over the fabric again, and fold the

triangles of fabric to the back of the board, securing them with masking tape. Next, fold in the outer edges of fabric, mitring the corners and securing them with tape (see page 8).

Using tape or craft adhesive, secure your chosen photograph in position. Form the ribbon into a loop, and secure it to the back of the frame with adhesive. To neaten the back of the frame, cut a piece of white card to the same size as the frame and secure it to the frame with adhesive.

PIERROT ▼		DMC	ANCHOR	MADEIRA
■	Black	310	403	Black
·	White	White	2	White
‖	Medium steel grey	317	400	1714
●	Light red	350	11	0213
Z	Medium shell grey	152	906	1807
ꟷ	Light shell grey	453	375	1806
╱	Pale grey	415	398	1803
	Rich red*	817	9046	0211

Note: bks the eyebrows with black; use medium shell grey for the face, and rich red* (*used for bks only) for the lips.

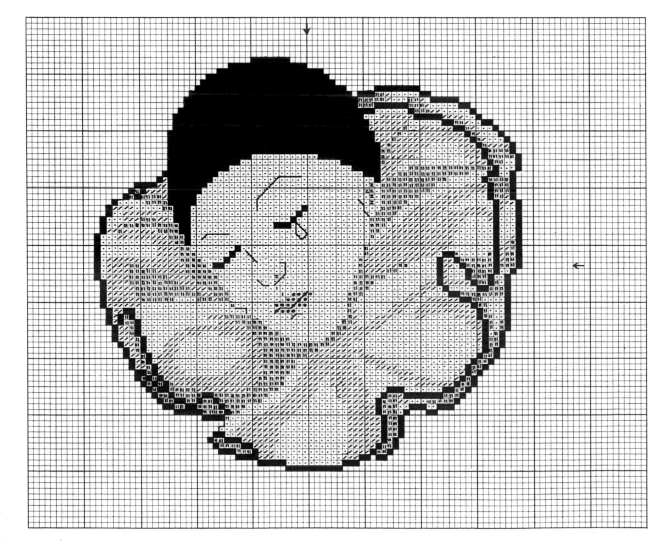

Greetings Cards

If you sit quietly by the riverside on a summer's day, you may observe the small brown dipper bobbing up and down searching for water insects, the swallow catching its food on the wing, or even the vivid colours of the kingfisher.

GREETINGS CARDS

YOU WILL NEED

For either the Kingfisher or the Dipper card, each
measuring 20cm × 15cm (8in × 6in), with an oval
cut-out measuring 14.5cm × 9.5cm (5³⁄₄in × 3³⁄₄in),
or for the Swallow card, measuring
20cm × 15.5cm (8in × 6¹⁄₄in), with a cut-out
measuring 12.5cm (5in) square:

20cm × 15cm (8in × 6in) of cream,
18-count Aida fabric
20cm × 15cm (8in × 6in) of iron-on interfacing
Stranded embroidery cotton and blending filament in
the colours given in the appropriate panel
No26 tapestry needle
Greetings card (for suppliers, see page 256)

•

THE EMBROIDERY

For each card, find the centre of your piece of Aida,
and start your embroidery from the centre of the
design. Work all the cross stitches first and then add
the backstitching. Use two strands of cotton for the
cross stitch, except where a metallic thread is indicated. In this case, use one strand of cotton together
with one strand of metallic thread. For the backstitching, use one strand of cotton. Gently steam
press on the wrong side when complete.

SWALLOW ▶			
(Hirundo rustica)	DMC	ANCHOR	MADEIRA
◩ Black	310	403	Black
◲ Pale grey	415	398	1803
⊟ White	White	1	White
1 Dark orange	920	339	0312
2 Orange	921	349	0311
⊟ Navy	939	127	1009
C Light iridescent blue	775	128	1001
Kr. 001 (Kreinik silver blending filament)			
◹ Dark grey blue	930	922	1712
◩ Grey blue	931	921	1711
∧ Light grey blue	932	920	1710
+ Pale orange	722	323	0307
X Cream	712	387	2101
▽ Fawn	613	956	2109
☰ Grey	413	401	1713
▲ Light navy	823	150	1008

Note: bks the eye highlight in white; the fly in black; the tail
in navy; the edge of the wing in fawn, and the eye outline in pale
grey.

ASSEMBLING THE CARDS

Iron the interfacing to the back of the embroidery,
and trim both to measure about 12mm (¹⁄₂in) larger
all around than the cut-out window.

Open out the self-adhesive mount and centre the
embroidery behind the aperture. Fold the card and
press firmly to secure. Some cards may require a dab
of glue to ensure a secure and neat finish.

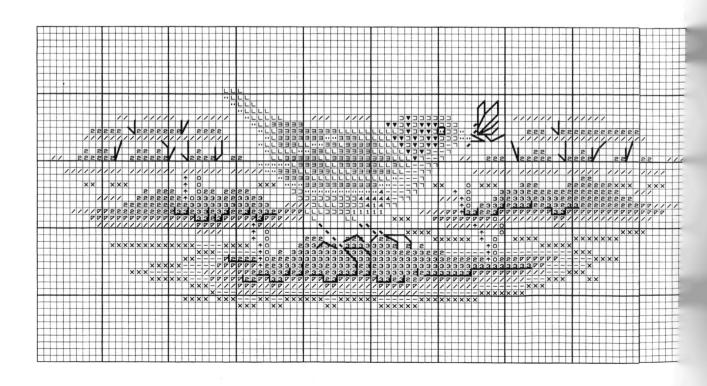

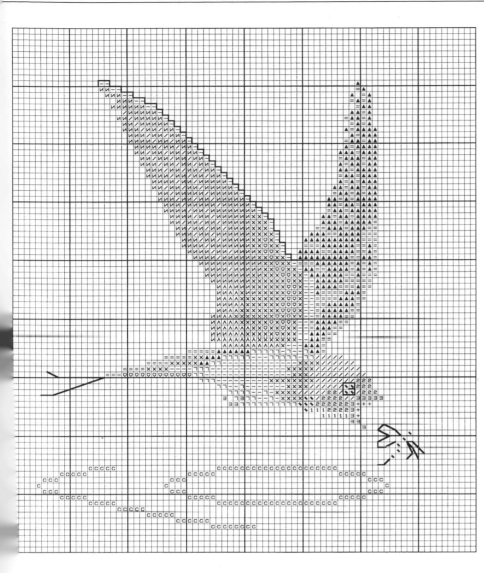

Note: bks the eye highlight in white, and the eye outline in pale grey.

Note: bks the fly, the beak and detail on the rocks in very dark brown; the bird's feet in grey; the grass between the rocks in green, and the eye in pale grey.

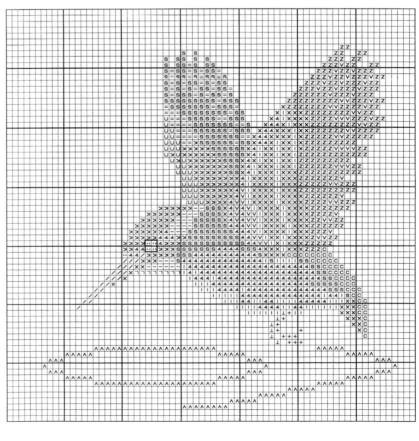

Clothes Brush and Towel

This clothes brush and towel, with the design of cute and cuddly West Highland Whites and Scottish Terriers, would make a lovely addition to any bathroom.

CLOTHES BRUSH
AND TOWEL

YOU WILL NEED

For the Clothes Brush, with a working area of
15cm × 3cm (6in × 1¼in), and a design area
of 12.5cm × 2cm (5in × ¾in), or
88 stitches by 14 stitches:

23cm × 11.5cm (9¼in × 4½in) of sky blue,
18-count Aida fabric
Stranded embroidery cotton in the colours given in
the appropriate panel
No26 tapestry needle
18cm × 6cm (7¼in × 2⅜in) of lightweight iron-on
interfacing
Purchased clothes brush (for suppliers,
see page 256)

For the Towel, with a working area of
27cm × 6.5cm (10¾in × 2½in), and a design
area of 18cm × 4cm (7¼in × 1½in):

Purchased towel, measuring 28cm × 46cm
(11 in × 18 in) (for suppliers, see page 256)
Stranded embroidery cotton in the colours given in
the appropriate panel
No26 tapestry needle

THE EMBROIDERY

For the clothes brush, prepare the edges of the fabric
and mark the central horizontal and vertical design
lines with basting stitches. Stretch the fabric in a
frame, following the instructions on page 5. Start the
embroidery at the centre of the design, using two
strands of thread in the needle for the cross stitch,
and one strand for the backstitch.

For the towel, baste the central horizontal and
vertical design lines of the Aida area and stretch it
in a frame. Start the embroidery at the centre of the
design, using three strands of thread in the needle
for the cross stitch, and one strand for the backstitch. Gently steam press the finished embroideries
on the wrong side.

MAKING UP

For the clothes brush, remove the basting stitches
and iron the interfacing to the wrong side of the
embroidery. Placing the acetate inset from the top of
the brush over the embroidery, draw around the

inset, ensuring that the design is central. Carefully
cut out the embroidery. Replace the acetate in the
brush, and place the embroidery on top, with the
right side facing the acetate. Re-assemble the brush
top. Using a small hammer, with a soft piece of cloth
covering the hammer-head to protect the brush rim,
tap the nails into the wood.

To complete the towel, simply remove the basting
stitches.

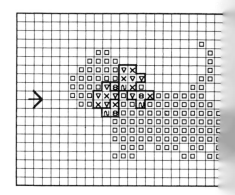

TOWEL ▼		DMC	ANCHOR	MADEIRA
■	Black	310	403	Black
□	White	White	2	White
X	Red	817	47	0211
8	Green	989	256	1401
▽	Blue	798	131	0911
Ⅳ	Yellow	726	295	0109

Note: bks bow outlines on black dogs in white, and bow outlines on
white dogs in black.

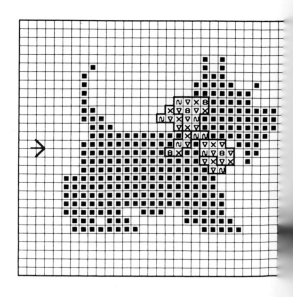

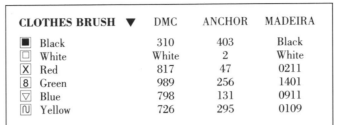

CLOTHES BRUSH ▼	DMC	ANCHOR	MADEIRA
■ Black	310	403	Black
□ White	White	2	White
X Red	817	47	0211
8 Green	989	256	1401
▽ Blue	798	131	0911
∩ Yellow	726	295	0109

Note: bks bow outlines on black dogs in white, and bow outlines on white dogs in black.

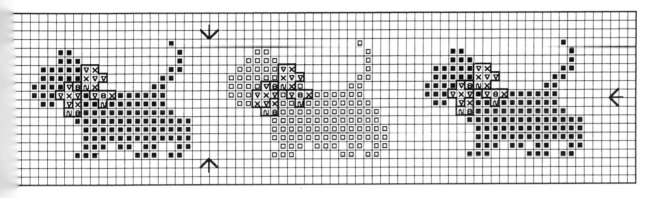

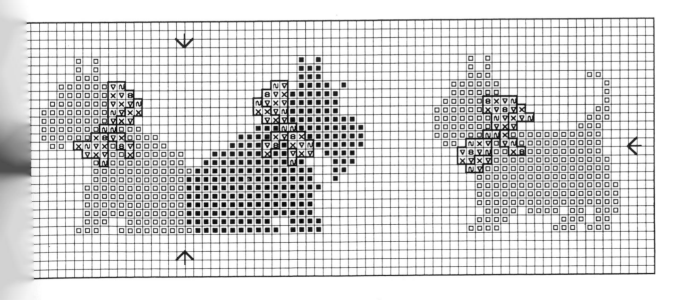

Fairytale Cards

Fun to stitch and a joy to receive, a card is a lovely gift to make a child feel special. You could use any of these attractive designs for a birthday, a 'get well' token, or perhaps just to send your love to a faraway grandchild.

FAIRYTALE CARDS

YOU WILL NEED

For each Card with an oval aperture measuring
12.5cm x 9cm (5in × 3½in):

17.5cm × 12.5cm (7in × 5in) of cream,
14-count Aida fabric
Stranded embroidery cotton in the colours given
in the appropriate panel
No26 tapestry needle
Card with an aperture as specified above,
for suppliers see page 256

•

THE EMBROIDERY

Prepare the fabric as described on page 5; find the centre by folding the fabric in half and then in half again, and lightly pressing the folded corner, or by marking the horizontal and vertical lines with basting stitches in a light-coloured thread. Mount the fabric in a hoop (see page 5) and start the embroidery at the centre of the design.

Following the chart, complete all the cross-stitching, using two strands of thread in the needle. These designs contains three-quarter stitches (see page 7), which are shown on the chart by the smaller symbols, and should be stitched in the corners indicated. Backstitch the outline, using one strand of navy blue thread. For the elf picture, stitch the needle with two strands of thread, and for his sewing cotton attach one strand of thread to the top of the boot and the bottom of the needle.

MOUNTING AND FRAMING

Remove the finished embroidery from the frame and remove any basting stitches. Wash if necessary, then press lightly on the wrong side, using a steam iron. Keeping the design centred, trim the embroidery to measure about 12mm (½in) larger all around than the size of the card window. Position the embroidery behind the window; open out the self-adhesive mount; fold the card, and press firmly to secure it. Some cards require a dab of glue to ensure a secure and neat finish.

SLEEPING BEAUTY ▶		ANCHOR	DMC	MADEIRA
▱	Pale orange	302	743	0113
·	Pale peach	8	353	0304
∷	Medium peach	9	352	0303
▬	Red	46	666	0210
◇	Medium brown	349	3776	2310
‖	Medium green	226	702	1306
X	Purple	111	552	0713
●	Royal blue	133	796	0913
■	Navy blue	127	939	1009

Note: bks around the outline, using one strand of navy blue thread in the needle.

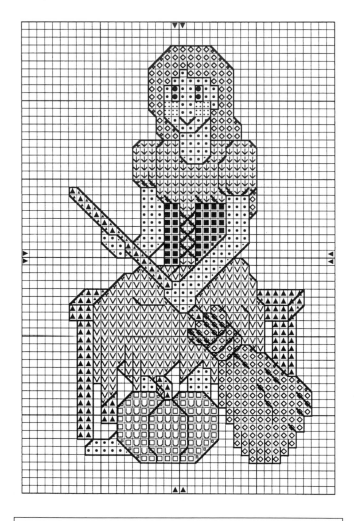

CINDERELLA ▲		ANCHOR	DMC	MADEIRA
·	Pale peach	8	353	0304
∷	Medium peach	9	352	0303
U	Medium orange	303	742	0114
▢	Deep orange	304	741	0202
◇	Medium brown	349	3776	2310
▲	Warm brown	352	300	2304
↓	Grass green	255	907	1410
V	Lilac	98	553	0712
●	Royal blue	133	796	0913
■	Navy blue	127	939	1009

Note: bks around the outline, using one strand of navy blue thread in the needle.

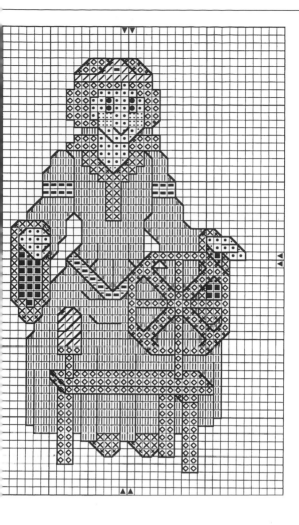

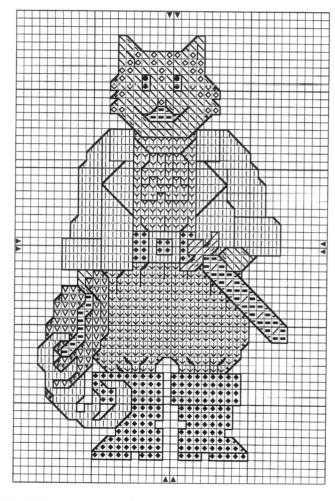

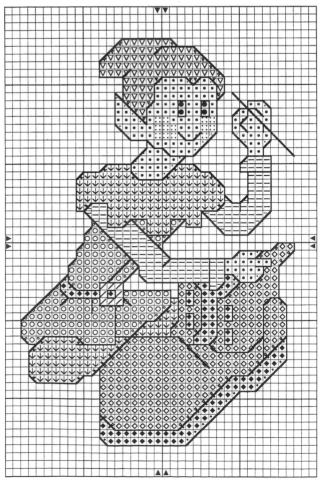

ANIMAL FRIENDS

These animal designs will appeal to all lovers of animals. Whether you admire large gentle plough horses, flamboyant and colourful cockerels, or mischievous puppies, there will be a cross stitch design for you to stitch in this chapter.

Fireside Cushions

This delightful pair of cushions with their amusing scenes show puppies snoozing in front of the fire. These bright and cheerful cushions will bring warmth to any room, and would look delightful decorating a child's bedroom.

Cow and Calf Traycloth

The mother and her young baby in this charming study of a cow and calf are stitched in rich creamy browns and set in a formal border of bright cornflowers.

COW AND CALF TRAYCLOTH

YOU WILL NEED

For the Traycloth, with a design area measuring 29cm × 22cm (11¼in × 8¾in), on a traycloth measuring 42cm × 34.5cm (16½in × 13½in):

*50cm × 44cm (20in × 17½in) of ivory,
27-count evenweave fabric
Stranded embroidery cotton in the colours given
in the appropriate panel
No24 tapestry needle
Matching sewing thread*

•

THE EMBROIDERY

Take the fabric to be used for the embroidery and prepare it as described on page 5; find the centre by folding, and mark the horizontal and vertical centre lines with basting stitches in a light-coloured thread. Set the fabric in a frame and count out from the centre to start stitching at a point convenient to you.

Complete the cross stitching first, using two strands of thread in the needle; take each stitch over two strands of fabric in each direction and make sure that all top stitches run in the same direction. Continue with the backstitching, using one strand of dark brown thread in the needle to outline the body of the cow.

Remove the embroidery from the frame. Gently handwash the finished piece, if necessary, and lightly press with a steam iron on the wrong side.

FINISHING THE TRAYCLOTH

Keeping the embroidery centred, trim the cloth to measure 44.5cm × 37cm (17½in × 14½in). Using matching thread, neaten the raw edges with machine zigzag, then turn under a 12mm (½in) hem and machine around all sides.

For an alternative, more traditional finish, you might choose to finish the edges with a fringe, held with hemstitching. For this you will need one skein of stranded cotton, to match the fabric. Trim the cloth, as above, then remove a thread of fabric at the hemline, 12mm (½in) in from the raw edge. Using two strands of cotton in the needle, and taking each stitch around either three or four threads of the fabric, hemstitch around the traycloth, along the

hemline, as shown on page 68. When you have finished, remove the weft threads below the hemstitching, to make a fringe.

HEMSTITCH

Bring the needle out on the right side, two threads below the drawn-thread line. Working from the left to right, pick up threads, as shown in the diagram. Bring the needle out again and insert it behind the fabric, to emerge two threads down, ready to make the next stitch. Before inserting the needle, pull the thread tight, so that the bound threads form a neat group.

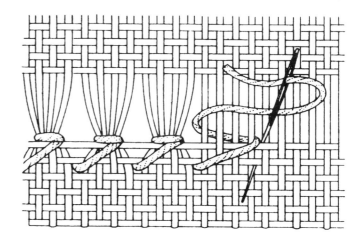

COW AND CALF ▶		ANCHOR	DMC	MADEIRA
⊢	Sand	942	738	2013
⊞	Light golden brown	1045	437	2012
⊤	Rich brown	310	434	2009
⊣	Grey	8581	646	1812
⊻	Grass green	265	471	1501
⊠	Purple	97	209	0803
·	White	1	White	White
Ɩ	Dark sand	943	436	2011
☐	Golden brown	1046	435	2010
■	Dark brown	382	3371	2004
⊟	Pink	893	225	0814
▪	Blue	176	809	0909
⊞	Dark green	268	580	1608

Note: bks around the cow and calf in dark brown.

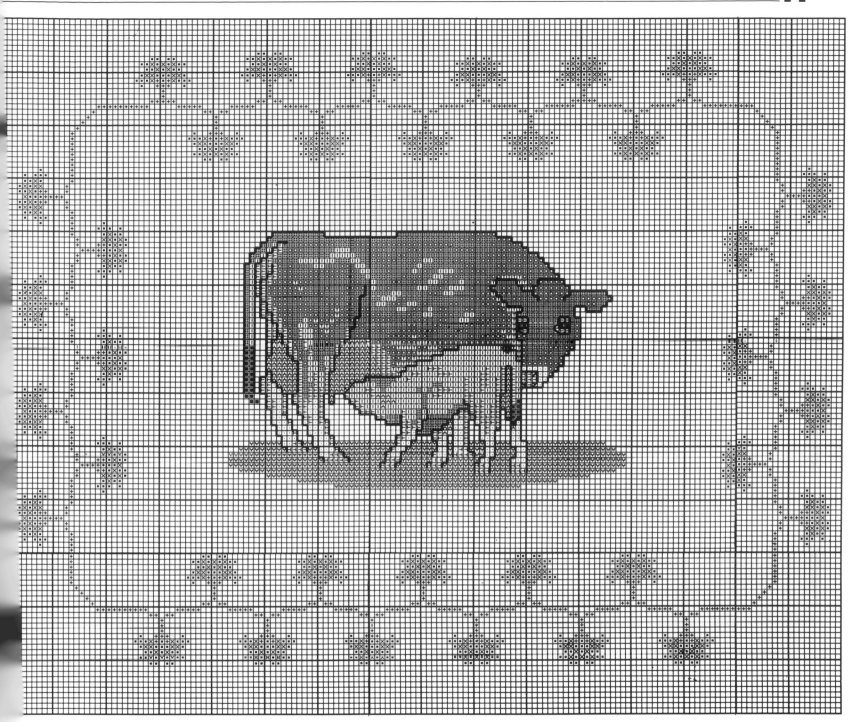

Mille-Fleurs Footstool

This elegant footstool would make a delightful and useful addition to a home, and could well become a talking point when guests come to call. The design is based on Flemish tapestries of the 16th century, mille-fleurs meaning 'many flowers'.

MILLE-FLEURS FOOTSTOOL

YOU WILL NEED

For the Footstool, with an inner frame measurement of 30cm × 38cm (12in × 15¼in), and design area of 20cm × 28cm (8in × 11¼in), or 144 stitches by 198 stitches:

50cm × 58cm (20in × 23¼in) of navy, 18-count Aida fabric
Stranded embroidery cotton in the colours given in the panel
No26 tapestry needle
Footstool (for suppliers, see page 256)
50cm × 58cm (20in × 23¼in) of navy, lightweight cotton fabric, for lining (optional)
Matching sewing thread
Strong thread, for lacing across the back

•

THE EMBROIDERY

Prepare the fabric, basting the central horizontal and vertical design lines, and stretch it in a frame, following the instructions on page 5. Start the embroidery at the centre of the design, using two strands of thread in the needle, and stitching over one block of fabric. Gently steam press the finished embroidery on the wrong side.

MAKING UP THE FOOTSTOOL

If the footstool pad is covered with pale fabric, it will be necessary to line the embroidery before making up the footstool. With right sides together and matching edges, pin and baste the lining fabric to the embroidery. Taking a 12mm (½in) seam allowance, stitch around the sides leaving a 15cm (6in) opening in the middle of one side. Trim the corners. Turn the embroidery right-side out, slip-stitch the opening to secure, and press. If lining is unnecessary, turn a 12mm (½in) hem on the embroidered fabric.

Undo the screws of the footstool base. Mark the centre sides of the pad and the embroidery with pins. Matching the centre points, and checking that the design is centred on the top of the pad, lace in position as illustrated on page 9. Replace the pad in the footstool base and tighten the screws.

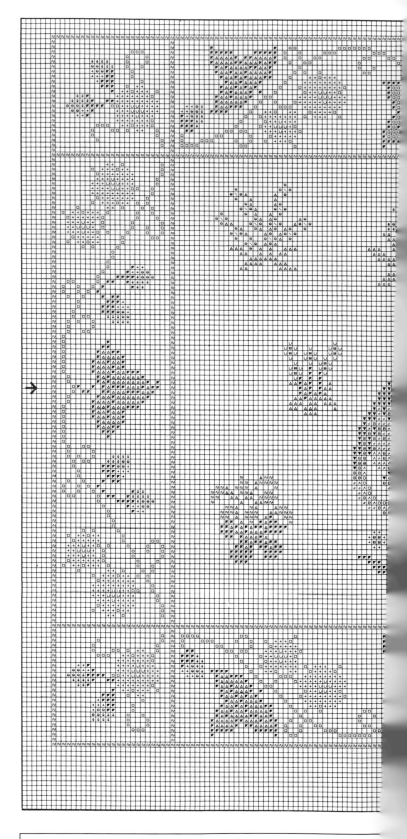

MILLE-FLEURS FOOTSTOOL ▲		DMC	ANCHOR	MADEIRA
▼	Dark tan	420	375	2104
⁄	Medium tan	3828	373	2103
8	Light tan	422	367	2102
Λ	Dark honey	3046	887	2206
O	Light honey	3047	852	2205
+	Cream	712	926	1707
■	Black	310	403	Black

		DMC	ANCHOR	MADEIRA			DMC	ANCHOR	MADEIRA
━	Red	321	13	0510	□	Medium green	988	257	1402
Ħ	Dark yellow	725	297	0108	△	Light green	989	256	1401
U	Yellow	726	295	0109	＼	White	White	2	White
→	Blue	334	977	1003	⊖	Medium pink	352	9	0303
ᴎ	Light blue	3325	144	1002	⬥	Dark pink	350	11	0213
1	Very light blue	775	975	1001					
ꜰ	Dark green	987	258	1403					

Key Box
and
Key Rack

If you are forever misplacing your keys, this key box and rack could provide the ideal solution to the problem, while making a delightful addition to your home.

KEY BOX
AND KEY RACK

YOU WILL NEED

For the Key Box, with a working area of
20cm × 25cm (8in × 10in), and a design area
of 12.5cm × 17.5cm (5in × 7in), or
71 stitches by 98 stitches:

28cm × 33cm (11¼in × 13¼in) of cream,
14-count Aida fabric
Stranded embroidery cotton in the colours given
in the appropriate panel
No26 tapestry needle
Purchased key box (for suppliers, see page 256)
21.5cm × 26.5cm (8½in × 10½in) of iron-on
interfacing (optional)
Strong thread, for lacing across the back

For the Key Rack, with a working area of
10cm × 10cm (4in × 4in), and a design area
of 7cm × 7.5cm (2¾in × 3in), or
49 stitches by 56 stitches:

19cm × 19cm (7½in × 7½in) of sky blue,
18-count Aida fabric
Stranded embroidery cotton in the colours given
in the appropriate panel
No26 tapestry needle
Purchased key rack (for suppliers, see page 256)
12cm × 12cm (4¾in × 4¾in) of iron-on
interfacing (optional)
Strong thread, for lacing across the back

•

THE EMBROIDERY

Prepare the edges of the fabric, and baste the central horizontal and vertical design lines. Stretch the
fabric in a frame, following the instructions on page
5. For the key box, start the embroidery just left of
centre, on the dog's head, counting carefully to
ensure correct placement. Use two strands of
thread in the needle for the cross stitch and one
strand for the backstitch. Complete the bottom left
area of the design, then carefully count up and
across to continue on the top right of the design.
For the key rack, start the embroidery in the
centre. Gently steam press the finished embroideries on the wrong side.

MAKING UP

You can either lace the embroidery over the card
provided by the manufacturer, or use iron-on interfacing as described below. For both items, mark the
centre lines on the card template provided. If you
prefer to use iron-on interfacing, lightly mark the
centre lines with pencil on the back of the embroidery and on the interfacing, and remove the basting
stitches. Iron a piece of interfacing to the back of
each embroidery, aligning the pencil marks. If you
are not using interfacing, leave the basting stitches
in at this stage.

To complete the assembly of both the key box and
key rack, lay the embroidery face-down with the template on top then, matching centre lines, draw around
the template using a soft pencil. Draw a second line
about 4cm (1½in) outside the first line and cut along
this outer line. For the key box, lace as shown on
page 9. To lace the key rack, make a line of running
stitches about 2cm (¾in) in from the raw edge, following the marked line. Place the card on the wrong
side and pull up the thread, spacing the gathers
evenly. Secure the gathering thread. Lace the back of
the embroidery in a clockwise fashion, starting at 12,
then down to 6, back to 1, and then down to 7, etc. If
using interfacing, carefully cut out the embroidery
along the template pencil line, and complete the
assembly.

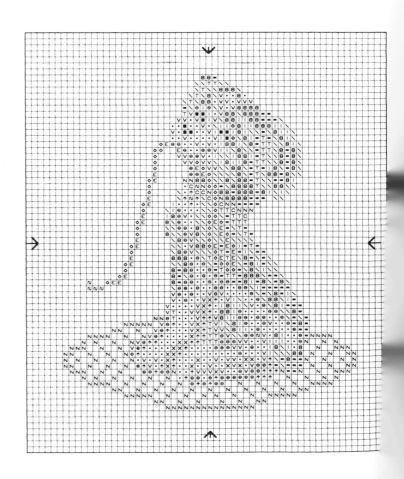

KEY RACK ◄		DMC	ANCHOR	MADEIRA
⊡	Very light tan	3776	347	2302
◺	Light tan	301	349	2306
▨	Medium tan	400	351	2305
◼	Dark tan	300	352	2304
◹	Very dark tan	801	359	2007
◻	White	White	2	White
▨	Cream	746	926	0101
◪	Dark cream	677	886	2207
◙	Beige	739	368	2014
◼	Black	310	403	Black
◩	Blue	793	131	0911
◧	Dark blue	797	132	0912
◨	Light gold	3047	852	2205
◪	Dark gold	3046	887	2206
◩	Green	988	257	1402
◪	Dark green	987	258	1403

KEY BOX ▲		DMC	ANCHOR	MADEIRA
1	Very light tan	3776	347	2302
\	Light tan	301	349	2306
8	Medium tan	400	351	2305
−	Dark tan	300	352	2304
T	Very dark tan	801	359	2007
·	White	White	2	White
V	Cream	746	926	0101
X	Dark cream	677	886	2207
⊖	Beige	739	368	2014
■	Black	310	403	Black
▲	Warm brown	838	380	1914
N	Blue	793	131	0911
C	Dark blue	797	132	0912
⋒	Gold	3047	852	2205
↑	Dark gold	3046	887	2206

Note: bks dog in very light tan, and bird and tree in warm brown.

Washdays' Peg Bag

These naughty puppies playing havoc with the washing will bring a touch of sunshine to any washday, and make a delightful and amusing embroidery to decorate this practical peg bag.

WASHDAYS' PEG BAG

YOU WILL NEED

For the Peg Bag, measuring 30cm × 35cm (12in × 14in) excluding coat hanger hook, with a design area of 21.5cm × 15cm (8¼in × 6in), or 120 stitches by 86 stitches:

Two pieces of 30cm × 23cm (12in × 9¼in) cream, 14-count Aida fabric
Stranded embroidery cotton in the colours given in the panel
No26 tapestry needle
Cotton perlé thread, DMC 436 or equivalent, for washing line
29cm × 21.5cm (11½in × 8¼in) of lightweight iron-on interfacing
2.5m (2½yd) of contrasting bias binding, 2.5cm (1in) wide
Matching sewing thread
30cm × 35cm (12in × 14in) of heavy cotton fabric, for backing
Coat hanger, 28cm (11¼) wide
50cm (20in) of ribbon, 10mm (⅜in) wide, to match bias binding

•

THE EMBROIDERY

Taking one of the pieces of Aida fabric, prepare the edges and mark the central horizontal and vertical design lines with basting stitches. Stretch the fabric in a frame, following the instructions on page 5. Start the embroidery at the centre of the design, using two strands of thread in the needle for the cross stitch, and one strand for the backstitch. When the backstitching is complete, use the cotton perlé thread to straight stitch the washing line. Gently steam press the finished embroidery on the wrong side.

MAKING UP

Remove the basting stitches from the embroidered fabric. Place the fabric and interfacing wrong sides together, and iron the interfacing in place. Attach the bias binding to the top edge, pin, baste, and machine stitch to the wrong side of the fabric, matching raw edges. Fold the binding to the right side and topstitch in position. Take the second piece of unstitched Aida fabric and make a double

12mm (½in) hem along one long edge (this is the bottom edge). Lay the piece of heavy cotton fabric backing, right side down, on a flat surface; lay the unembroidered piece of Aida fabric over this, right side up, matching top edges, and pin in position. Mark the centre position of the coat hanger hook with a basting stitch. Place the embroidered Aida, right side up, on top of both the backing fabric and the unembroidered Aida section, and align with the bottom edges of the backing fabric. Pin in position.

To round off the corners of the fabric, place a cup against each corner and lightly mark the fabric with a pencil. Trim off the excess corner fabric. Baste *all* layers together. Add the bias binding all the way around, as described above, leaving a small opening for the coat hanger hook. Topstitch the bias binding from the right side, carefully following the edge, and leaving the opening for the hook. Press the completed peg bag. Slip the coat hanger inside the top section and up through the opening. To finish, add a ribbon bow.

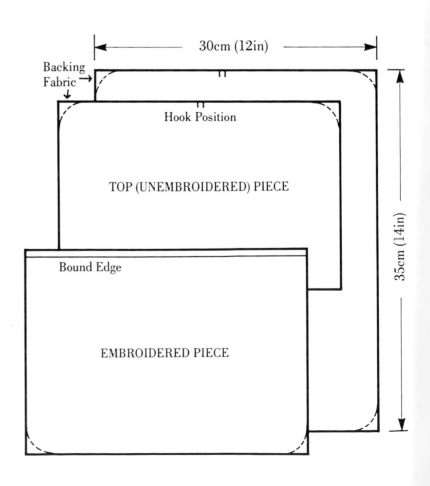

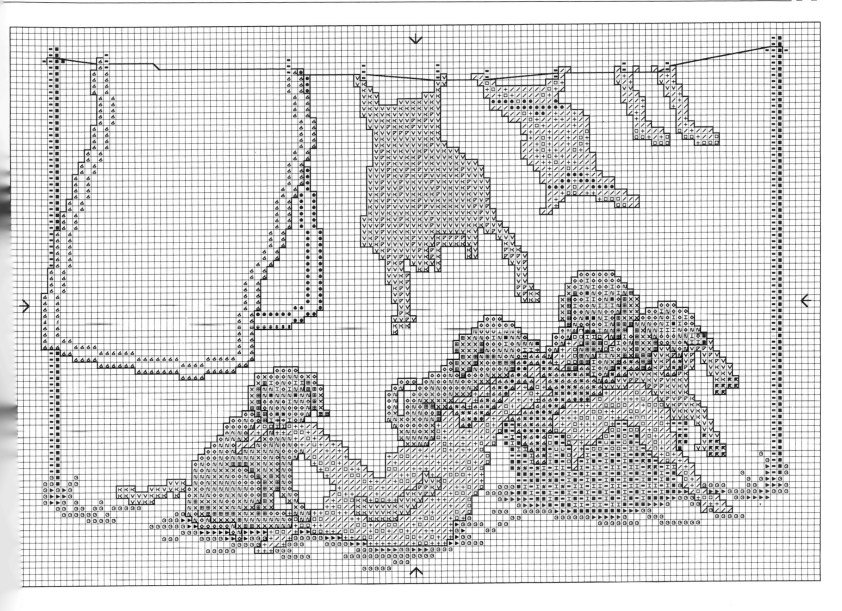

WASHDAYS'
PEG BAG ▲

		DMC	ANCHOR	MADEIRA			DMC	ANCHOR	MADEIRA
I	Ivory	822	390	1908	✗	Medium pink	760	9	0405
◇	Cream	739	366	2014	G	Medium green	3347	266	1408
N	Caramel	738	361	2013	▶	Dark green	3345	268	1406
X	Medium caramel	437	362	2012	▽	Dark blue	322	978	1004
⊞	Dark caramel	436	363	2011	•ǀ•	Beige	841	378	1911
▬	Brown	869	944	2105	╱	White	White	2	White
■	Dark brown	3031	360	2003	⊞	Very light grey	762	397	1804
□	Grey	415	398	1803		Medium grey*	318	398	1802
V	Light blue	3755	161	1013					
⊼	Very dark blue	312	979	1005					
K	Medium blue	334	977	1003					
6	Light pink	761	8	0404					
•	Dark pink	3712	10	0406					

Note: bks pink washing with medium pink, blue washing with dark blue, white washing with medium grey, and puppies with dark caramel (*used for backstitch only).*

Cockerel Cushion

This proud fellow – a true king of the farmyard – is richly designed, with threads of different textures on a subtle peach background. Here, he has been made into a cushion cover, but he could be framed as a picture.

COCKEREL CUSHION

YOU WILL NEED

For the Cockerel Cushion, measuring
37cm (14½in) square, with a design area of
25.5cm (10in) square:

47cm (18½in) of peach, 25-count evenweave fabric
Stranded embroidery cotton in the colours given
in the panel
No24 tapestry needle
39.5cm (15½in) square of peach fabric,
for backing
2.3m (2½yd) of matching peach No2 piping cord
Matching sewing thread
38cm (15in) square cushion pad

NOTE: Anchor Marlitt polyester threads were used here to give a slight contrast in texture. The Madeira, Decora threads are also polyester; there is no DMC equivalent, though you might mix the stranded cottons suggested with blending filaments for a similar effect.

●

THE EMBROIDERY

Prepare the fabric as described on page 5; find the centre by folding, and mark the horizontal and vertical centre lines with basting stitches in a light-coloured thread. Set the fabric in a frame (see page 5) and count out from the centre to start stitching at a point convenient to you.

Complete the cross stitching, using two strands of the appropriate thread in the needle for all cross stitches. Take all cross stitches over two threads of fabric in each direction, and make sure that all top stitches run in the same direction. Finish with the backstitching, using one thread of stranded cotton in the needle.

Take the finished embroidery from the frame and remove any basting stitches. Wash if necessary, then press lightly on the wrong side, using a steam iron.

MAKING THE COVER

Keeping the embroidery centred, trim the fabric to measure 39.5cm (15½in) square. With right sides together and taking a 12mm (½in) seam allowance, machine stitch the backing fabric and the embroidered front cover together, leaving a 32cm (12½in) gap at one side. Trim across the seam allowance at corners to remove excess fabric; neaten raw edges, and turn the cover right side out.

Insert the cushion pad, and slipstitch the opening, but still leave a small 2.5cm (1in) opening. Slipstitch piping cord around the edge of the cushion, inserting the ends into the remaining small opening, then slipstitch the opening.

COCKEREL ▶		ANCHOR	DMC	MADEIRA
■	Black	403	310	Black
+	Bright yellow	291	444	0106
T	Orange	303	742	0114
I	Dark pink	11	350	0213
⊢	Light tan	1001	976	2302
▪	Tan	1004	920	0312
╵	Light purple	871	3042	0807
∷	Emerald green	209	912	1213
⌐	Rich emerald green	210	561	1206
·	White	1	White	White
✕	Dark green	268	580	1608
□	Yellow	295	726	0100
⊥	Grass green	266	470	1502
⊣	Red	13	321	0510
╱	Soft brown	349	301	2306
⊟	Dark purple	873	3740	0806
L	Pine	218	890	1314
◤	Dark bright green	1067 Marlitt	909	D1496
⊠	Rust	1003 Marlitt	943	D1495
Γ	Rich bright green	1066 Marlitt	3345	D1556
⊏	Dark green	853 Marlitt	319	D1570

Note: bks around beak and legs in pine, using one strand.

Autumn Harvest Picture

This delightful picture with its adorable puppy sitting in a basket would certainly appeal to any dog-lover, and receive a place of honour in any room in the home.

AUTUMN HARVEST PICTURE

For the Picture, with a design area of
16.5cm (6½in) square, or 93 stitches by
90 stitches:

25cm (10in) square of peach, 14-count Aida fabric
Stranded embroidery cotton in the colours given
in the panel
No26 tapestry needle
Strong thread, for lacing across the back
Card to fit frame recess, for mounting
Frame of your choice

•

THE EMBROIDERY

Prepare the fabric, and mark the central horizontal
and vertical design lines with basting stitches.
Sretch the fabric in a frame, following the
instructions on page 5. Start the embroidery at the
centre of the design, using two strands of thread in
the needle for the cross stitch, and one strand for
the backstitch. Gently steam press the finished
embroidery on the wrong side, leaving the basting
stitches in position.

MOUNTING

Use either of the methods described on page 9 to
lace and mount your finished embroidery. To achieve
a smooth finish, you may find it helpful to pin the
fabric to the edge of the board, to hold it in place.
Starting at the centre of each side, push the pins into
the board edge, stretching the fabric gently as you
go. Check that the grain of the fabric is straight, and
the embroidery is central, before lacing or fixing
with tape. Place the stretched embroidery in the
frame of your choice. If the frame has glass, use a
mount or place thin strips of card inside the frame
rebate to prevent the embroidery touching the glass.
As well as spoiling the look of the embroidery,
condensation might form on the inside of the glass
and cause mildew stains on your precious work.

AUTUMN HARVEST PICTURE ▶		DMC	ANCHOR	MADEIRA
■	Black	310	403	Black
▶	Very dark grey	844	401	1810
⊖	Dark grey	645	400	1811
△	Medium grey	647	8581	1813
L	Light grey	648	900	1814
1	Very light grey	3072	847	1805
╱	White	White	2	White
•	Very dark tan	801	359	2007
▬	Dark tan	433	358	2008
◆╎◆	Medium tan	435	365	2010
◇	Beige	739	366	2014
N	Light peach	3779	868	0404
X	Medium peach	758	9575	0403
⋈	Dark peach	3778	337	0402
U	Light tan	437	362	2012
H	Light green	472	253	1414
→	Medium green	471	265	1501
8	Dark green	470	266	1502
M	Dark pink	351	10	0214
+	Grey/beige	3782	388	1907

Note: bks leaf veins in very dark tan.

COUNTRY LIFE

The beauty and variety of the countryside and its wildlife are captured in these delightful cross stitch designs. The projects include a scene of the riverside, a view through a cherry tree, and even a leaping lamb picture frame.

THROUGH THE CHERRY TREE

YOU WILL NEED

For the Picture, set in a frame with an internal measurement of 30cm × 24.5cm (11½in × 9½in):

46cm × 38cm (18in × 15in) of cream,
11-count Aida fabric
Stranded embroidery cotton in the colours given in
the panel
No24 tapestry needle
Picture frame as specified above
Firm card, to fit the frame
Lightweight synthetic batting/wadding,
the same size as the card
Strong thread for mounting
Paper glue stick

•

THE EMBROIDERY

Prepare the fabric as described on page 5; find the centre either by folding the fabric in half and then in half again, and lightly pressing the folded corner, or by marking the horizontal and vertical centre lines with basting stitches in a light-coloured thread. Mount the fabric in a frame (see page 5) and start the design from the centre.

Following the chart, complete all the cross stitching first, using two strands of thread in the needle. Finish with the backstitching, again using two strands of thread. Be careful not to take dark threads across the back of the work in such a way that they show through on the right side.

The birds' eyes, indicated by black dots on the chart, can either be made with a single french knot, stitched with two strands of black thread, or you can use a small black bead for each eye.

MOUNTING AND FRAMING

Remove the finished embroidery from the frame and wash if necessary, then press lightly on the wrong side, using a steam iron. Take extra care when pressing if you have used beads for the eyes. Spread glue evenly on one side of the mounting card, and lightly press the batting to the surface. Lace the embroidery over the padded surface (see page 9). Remove basting stitches; place the mounted embroidery in the frame, and assemble the frame according to the manufacturer's instructions.

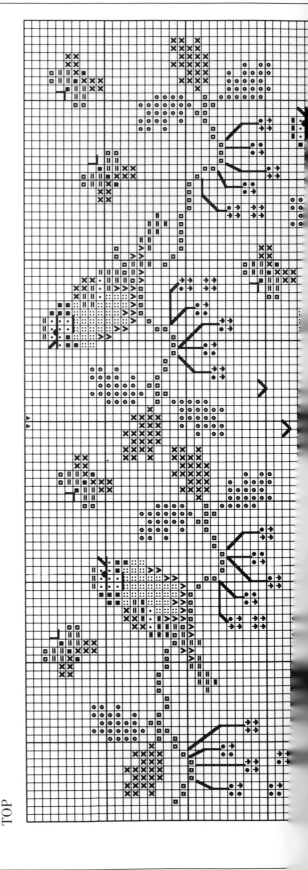

TOP

THROUGH THE CHERRY TREE ▲	ANCHOR	DMC	MADEIRA
• White	1	White	White
■ Black	403	Black	Black
= Blue	979	312	1005
∷ Light yellow green	278	472	1414
V Medium yellow green	280	733	1609

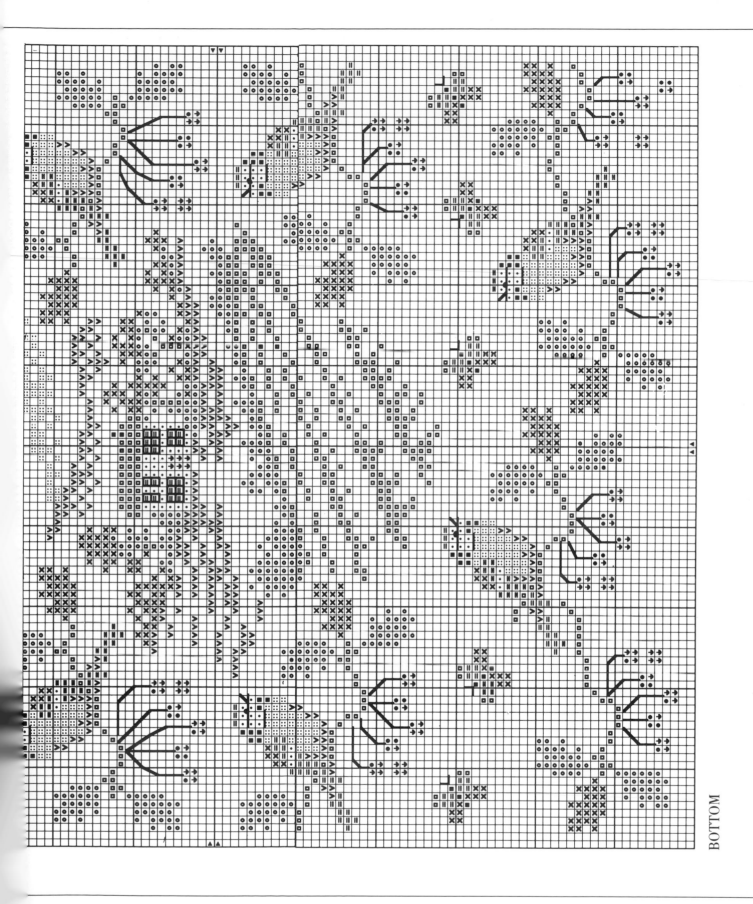

BOTTOM

		ANCHOR	DMC	MADEIRA
X	Medium green	267	580	1608
O	Dark green	268	935	1504
□	Dark brown	360	898	2006
●	Bright red	19	817	0212
↓	Deep red	20	498	0513

Note: bks cherry stems in dark green; blue tits' heads and beaks, birds in the sky and butterflies' antennae in black, and window outlines in medium yellow green; either use beads or french knots in two strands of black for blue tits' eyes.

River Scene

In the cool clear light of a summer morning, the grey heron stands motionless in shallow waters by the river's edge. The watchful bird waits patiently for a fish to surface – a potential meal for a hungry bird. The subtle colours offer an enjoyable challenge to the stitcher.

RIVER SCENE

YOU WILL NEED

For the Picture, mounted in a rectangular landscape frame, with a coloured mount 4cm (1½in) deep, with an aperture measuring 22.5cm × 18cm (8¾in × 7in):

40.5cm × 38cm (16in × 15in) of pale blue, 14-count Aida fabric
Stranded embroidery cotton in the colours given in the panel
No24 tapestry needle
Strong thread, for lacing across the back when mounting
Stiff cardboard, for backing
Frame of your choice
Mount to fit the frame, with an aperture as specified above

●

THE EMBROIDERY

Prepare the fabric by marking the centre lines of the design with basting stitches. Start your embroidery from the centre of the design, completing the cross stitching first, and then the backstitching. Use three strands of thread for the cross stitches and two strands for the backstitching. Leaving the basting stitches in place, gently steam press the finished embroidery on the wrong side.

ASSEMBLING THE PICTURE

Using the basting stitches as guidelines, centre the picture over the cardboard mount, which should be cut to the size of the chosen frame. Lace the embroidery over the mount, following the instructions on page 9, and remove basting stitches. Insert the coloured mount into the frame and then the mounted embroidery; complete assembly of the frame according to the manufacturer's instructions.

GREY HERON							
(Ardea cinerea)	DMC	ANCHOR	MADEIRA		DMC	ANCHOR	MADEIRA
⊠ Medium grey	414	400	1801	↘ Light grey blue	932	920	1710
⊡ Pale grey	415	398	1803	⋀ Pale blue	928	274	1709
— White	White	1	White	↓ Orange	720	326	0309
⊟ Black	310	403	Black	← Light orange	722	323	0307
1 Dark fawn	840	379	1912	○ Dull green	3052	859	1509
2 Fawn	842	376	1910	△ Dark green	3362	862	1601
5 Yellow	743	297	0113	Y Green	3363	861	1602
V Grey blue	931	921	1711	· Light green	3364	843	1603

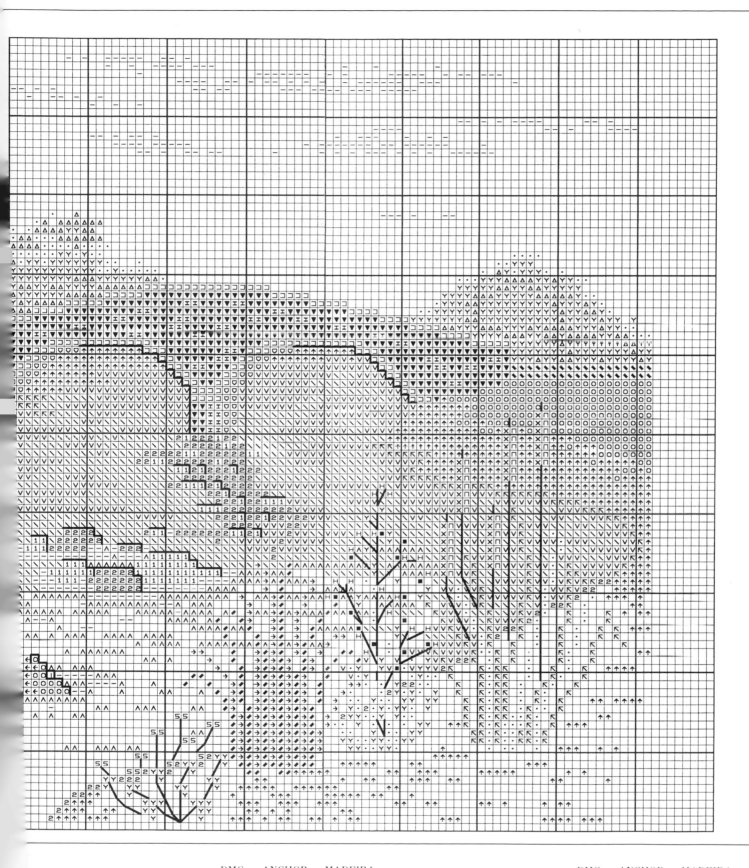

		DMC	ANCHOR	MADEIRA			DMC	ANCHOR	MADEIRA
◿	Bluish green	320	215	1311	⊥	Light mushroom	452	232	1807
◺	Dark dull green	3051	846	1508	▼	Pale mushroom	453	231	1806
→	Dark blue green	319	246	1313	H	Deep pink	602	63	0702
↑	Light dull green	3053	859	1510	■	Pink	603	62	0701
♡	Dark grey	413	401	1713					
⊓	Brown	898	360	2006					
X	Reddish brown	433	371	2008					
⊐	Mushroom	451	233	1808					

Note: bks the eye of the heron in orange; the fish's head and the flower stems in dark green; the heron's crest and the fish's mouth in black; the bullrush stalks in brown; the detail on the rocks, the bridge arches and the heron's head, neck and body in dark grey, and the fish's eye in yellow.

Fisherman's Log Book and Mug

Two ideal gifts for an angler –
a special log book in which to record
catches, and a large mug from which
to sip a warming brew, as he waits
for that 'really big one'.

FISHERMAN'S LOG BOOK AND MUG

YOU WILL NEED

For the Log Book, measuring 21.5cm × 15.5cm (8½in × 6in):

53cm × 30.5cm (21in × 12in) of cream, 18-count Aida fabric
47cm × 16.5cm (18½in × 6½in) of white interfacing
Stranded embroidery cotton in the colours given in the appropriate panel
No26 tapestry needle
A notebook of your choice

For the Fisherman's Mug, height 10cm (4in), diameter 8.5cm (3½in):

Stranded embroidery cotton in the colours given in the appropriate panel
No24 tapestry needle
Mug, available from needlework stockists complete with ready-cut piece of 14-count canvas (for suppliers, see page 256)

●

THE LOG BOOK

Fold the Aida in half, giving you a working area of 26.5cm × 30.5cm (10½in × 12in). With the fold on the left, measure in 12mm (½in) and baste from top to bottom. From this line, measure a further 15.5cm (6in) across and baste another, parallel line. Baste two horizontal lines 21.5cm (8½in) apart, equidistant from the top and bottom edges of your working area, leaving a rectangular area measuring 21.5cm × 15.5cm (8½in × 6in) for the front cover of your log book. Centre your embroidery in this area. Starting

from the centre, use two strands of cotton for the cross stitching, and two for backstitching. Steam press on the wrong side when complete.

Centre the interfacing on the Aida and fold in a narrow hem along all the edges, enclosing the interfacing. Machine stitch into position. Centre the book on the wrong side of the fabric and fold the extra width over the front and back side edges of the cover. Topstitch through the folds at the top and bottom to form pockets.

THE MUG

For the mug, find the centre of the canvas and start your embroidery from the centre of the design. Complete the cross stitching first, using three strands of thread and then the backstitching, using two.

Assemble the mug, following the manufacturer's instructions.

PERCH AND ROACH MUG ▼ *(Perca fluviatilis & Rutilus rutilus)*		DMC	ANCHOR	MADEIRA
◣	Black	310	403	Black
⊟	Cream	712	387	2101
⊡	Dark grey	844	1041	1810
6	Greeny yellow	734	280	1610
8	Grey blue	930	922	1712
T	Blue	932	920	1710
╱	Pale blue	928	274	1709
▽	Pale grey	762	397	1804
●	Deep pink	351	11	0214
⊥	Pink	352	9	0303
+	Orange	720	326	0309
Y	Light green	772	264	1604
II	Grey	645	273	1811
⊥	Brown yellow	834	874	2204
■	Pale pink	225	892	0814
	Yellow*	972	298	0107
	White*	White	1	White

Note: bks the eyes in yellow; the fins, gills, mouths and bubbles in dark grey; and the eye highlights in white* (*used for backstitching only).*

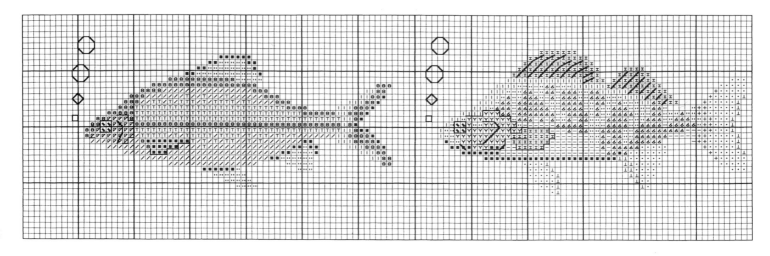

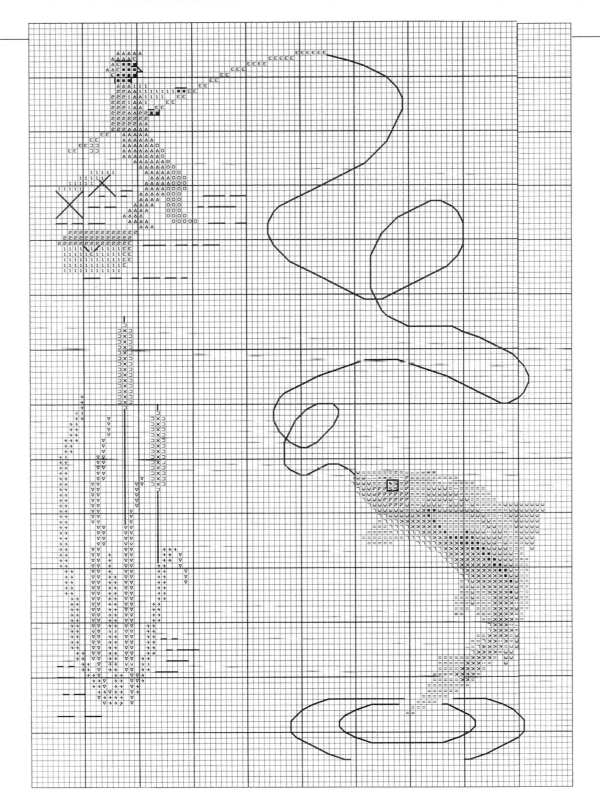

SALMON LOG BOOK ▲
(Salmo salar)

		DMC	ANCHOR	MADEIRA
⟍	Black	310	403	Black
⊓	Pale grey blue	928	274	1709
E	Dark brown	3031	905	2003
1	Ginger brown	680	901	2210
2	Gold	676	891	2208
5	Deep yellow	972	298	0107
=	Dark grey blue	924	851	1706
⊔	Grey blue	926	850	1707
⋈	Light grey blue	927	849	1708
▱	Pale grey	762	397	1804
▽	Dark green	520	862	1514
○	Dull green	3362	263	1601

		DMC	ANCHOR	MADEIRA
△	Light green	522	859	1513
→	Green	3363	261	1602
▮▮	Dark grey	844	1041	1810
X	Reddish brown	433	371	2008
⊐	Brown	898	360	2006
■	Pale pink	225	892	0814
	Pale blue*	775	128	1001

Note: bks the fish's eye in deep yellow; the fishing line, and the detail on man's hands and face in dark grey; the water in pale blue* (*used for backstitching only); the ground around the rushes and around the man in dark green; and the bullrush stems and detail on the basket and seat in dark brown.

Leaping Lamb Picture Frame

These little lambs are gambolling among poppies. The whites and bright reds are brought to life by the sky blue background – a photograph of your loved ones will complete the design.

LEAPING LAMB
PICTURE FRAME

YOU WILL NEED

For the Leaping Lamb Picture Frame, with
an internal measurement of 24cm × 29cm
(9¹⁄₂in × 11¹⁄₂in), and a cut-out as specified below:

36cm × 42cm (14in × 16¹⁄₂in) of pale blue,
14-count Aida fabric
Stranded embroidery cotton in the colours given
in the appropriate panel
No24 tapestry needle
Frame, as specified above
Mount to fit the frame, with a cut-out measuring
11.5cm × 16cm (4¹⁄₂in × 6¹⁄₄in) or to display your
favourite photograph
Masking tape and clear fabric glue

•

THE EMBROIDERY

Prepare the fabric as described on page 5; find
the centre by folding, and mark the horizontal and
vertical centre lines with basting stitches in a
light-coloured thread. Set the fabric in a frame and
count out from the centre to start stitching at a point
convenient to you.

Complete the cross stitching, using two strands of
thread in the needle and making sure that all top
stitches run in the same direction. Finish with the
backstitched outlines, using one strand of grey
thread in the needle.

Remove the embroidery from the frame. Gently
handwash the finished piece, if necessary, and
lightly press with a steam iron on the wrong side.

COMPLETING THE FRAME

Stretch and mount the embroidery over the
cardboard mount, mitring the corners and using
masking tape to hold the edges as explained on
page 9. Leaving a margin of 3cm (1¹⁄₄in) on all sides,
cut away spare fabric from the centre of the mount.
Snip diagonally into the corners, then bring the
edges of the fabric to the back of the mount and

again secure with masking tape. To prevent fraying
and hold the fabric securely, put a dab of glue at the
back of the mount on the inner corners.

Tape the photograph in place behind the mount
and insert the mounted picture into the frame.
Finish assembling the frame according to the
manufacturer's instructions.

Back view of mount showing centre cut and
ready to be taped back.

LEAPING LAMB ▶	ANCHOR	DMC	MADEIRA
⊥ Ecru	387	Ecru	1908
▦ Grey	399	414	1801
T Yellow	295	726	0100
⊢ Bright green	267	3346	1407
⊓ Dark pink	11	350	0213
· White	1	White	White
∷ Pale pink	25	3689	0607
□ Green	261	989	1401
■ Black	403	310	Black
▪ Red	13	321	0510

Note: bks around lambs in grey.

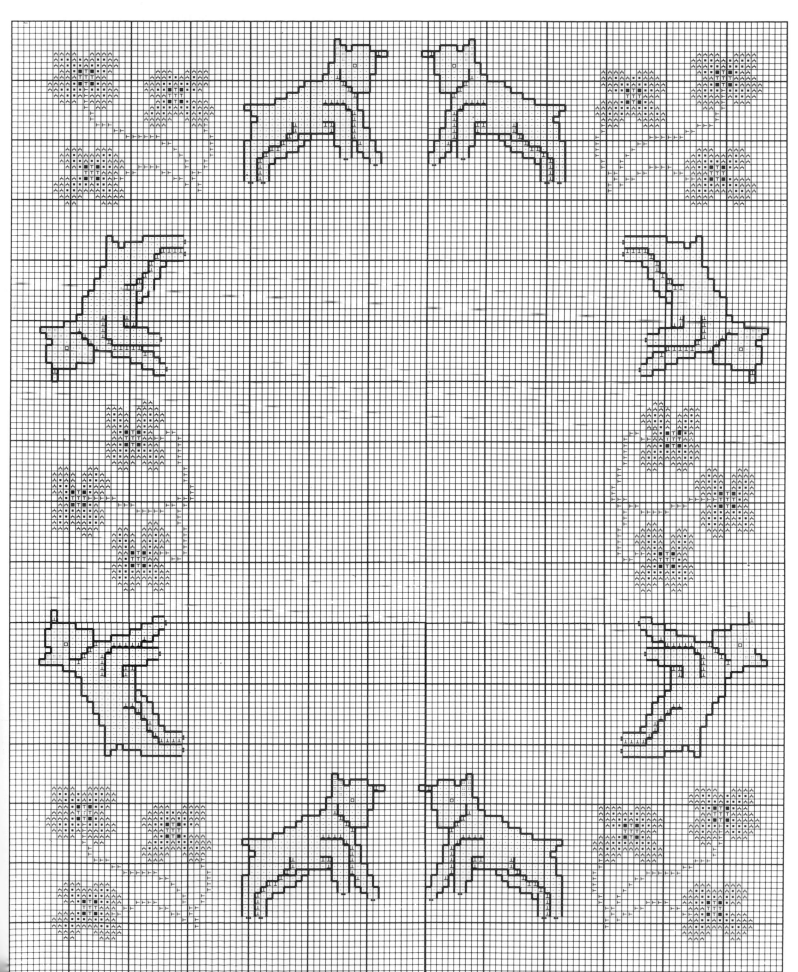

Duck Napkins

Ducks have a universal appeal.
The elegant and attractive pintail is
largely a winter visitor; the teal
is with us all year and is Britain's
smallest duck, while the larger
shelduck is found most often on the
tidal estuaries of rivers.

DUCK NAPKINS

YOU WILL NEED

For each Napkin, measuring 38cm (15in) square:

*38cm (15in) square of grey, 28-count evenweave
fabric (No429.79)
Stranded embroidery cotton in the colours given
in the appropriate panel
No26 tapestry needle*

•

THE EMBROIDERY

Baste a vertical line 6cm (2¼in) in from the left-hand side, and a horizontal one 6cm (2¼in) up from the lower edge. The point where these two lines intersect is the bottom left-hand corner of a 13cm (5in) square which will hold your chosen duck motif. Complete this square with basting stitches, and then find the centre point. Start your embroidery from the stitch nearest to this point. Care must be taken in counting, as you will be working over two fabric threads. Use two strands of cotton in the needle for both cross stitch and backstitch, except when back-stitching beaks and eye highlights, where one strand is used. Complete all the cross stitching before adding the backstitches. Gently steam press the finished embroidery on the wrong side.

FRINGING

On all four sides of your napkin, withdraw a single fabric thread 12mm (½in) in from the outer edge. The fringing can be secured in one of several ways: by machining around the square left by the withdrawn threads, using either straight stitch or narrow zigzag stitch, or by overcasting every alternate thread by hand.

When you have secured the line by your chosen method, remove all cross threads below the stitched line to complete the fringe. Alternatively, if a more hard-wearing edge is preferred, a folded and stitched hem can be used instead of fringing.

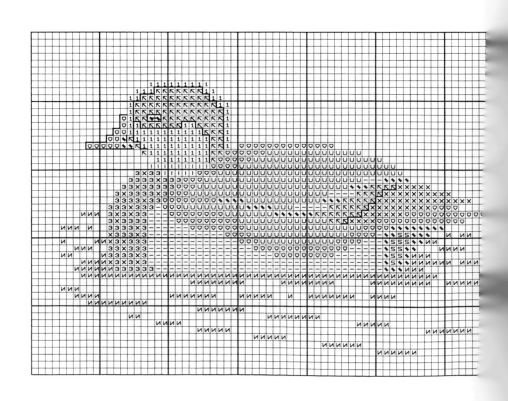

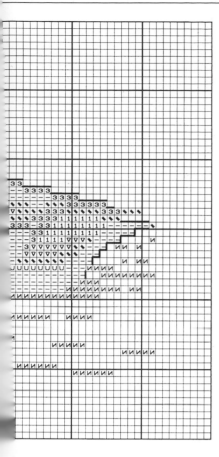

SHELDUCK ◄

(Tadorna tadorna)		DMC	ANCHOR	MADEIRA
◢	Black	310	403	Black
⊟	Ecru	Ecru	926	Ecru
1	Ginger	435	365	2010
2	Light ginger	436	363	2011
3	Oatmeal	543	276	1909
◹	Grey blue	926	850	1707
⋈	Red	347	13	0407
▽	Dark green	934	862	1506
▬	Green	936	269	1507
U	Fawn	842	376	1910

Note: bks the body of the duck in fawn, and the eye in ecru.

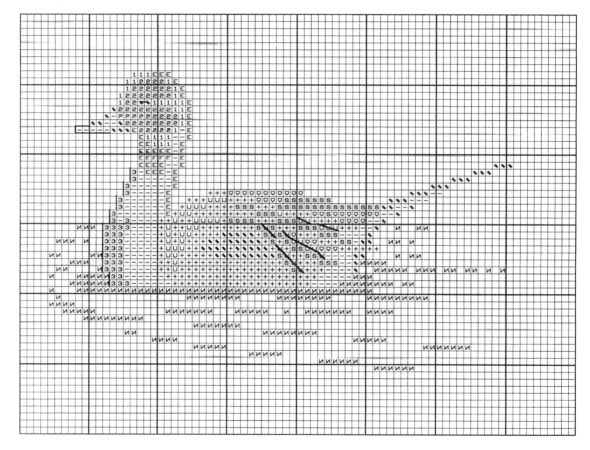

AL ◄

(as crecca)	DMC	ANCHOR	MADEIRA
Black	310	403	Black
Ecru	Ecru	926	Ecru
Chestnut	434	309	2009
Ginger	435	365	2010
Oatmeal	543	276	1909
Lemon	727	293	0110
Grey blue	926	850	1707
Green	937	268	1504
Light brown	840	379	1912
Fawn	642	392	1906
Light fawn	613	956	2109

*bks the beak of the duck in black, and the nostril, eye, head and
in ecru.*

PINTAIL ▲

(Anas acuta)		DMC	ANCHOR	MADEIRA
◢	Black	310	403	Black
⊟	Ecru	Ecru	926	Ecru
E	Chestnut	434	309	2009
1	Ginger	435	365	2010
2	Light ginger	436	363	2011
3	Oatmeal	543	276	1909
◹	Grey blue	926	850	1707
S	Brown	839	380	1913
♡	Light brown	840	379	1912
+	Fawny brown	841	378	1911
U	Fawn	842	376	1910

*Note: bks the duck's breast in fawn; the beak and wing feathers
in black, and the eye highlight in ecru.*

Frame and Trinket Box

Beside undisturbed lowland river banks, the water vole *(Arvicola terrestris)* spends its day feeding on waterside plants, swimming along the edge of the river or making its burrows near the bank.

FRAME AND TRINKET BOX

YOU WILL NEED

For the Frame, measuring 27cm × 22cm
(10³/₄in × 8³/₄in) internally with an aperture
measuring 14cm × 9cm (5¹/₂in × 3¹/₂in):

27cm × 22cm (10³/₄in × 8³/₄in) of white,
14-count perforated paper
Stranded embroidery cotton in the colours given
in the appropriate panel
No24 tapestry needle
27cm x 22cm (10³/₄in × 8³/₄in) of iron-on interfacing
Frame of your choice

For the Trinket Box, with a lid measuring
7.5cm (3in) in diameter:

12.5cm (5in) square of cream, 18-count Aida fabric
12.5cm (5in) square of iron-on interfacing
Stranded embroidery cotton in the colours given in
the appropriate panel
No26 tapestry needle
Trinket box (for suppliers, see page 256)

NOTE: *Trinket boxes are available with bowls*
made from wood, hand-cut crystal, silver-plate or
porcelain in a variety of colours. You may wish to
choose a bowl to match one of the colours
in the embroidery.

●

THE EMBROIDERY

For the frame, find the centre of the perforated paper
by counting the spaces between the holes. Mark this
point with a soft pencil, and then count out to a
convenient starting point on the border. Complete all
the cross stitches first, and then add the backstitching. Use three strands of embroidery cotton in the
needle for the cross stitching and two strands for the
backstitching.

For the trinket box, find the centre point on your
square of Aida and, beginning from the centre of the
pattern, embroider the motif, using two strands of
cotton in the needle for the cross stitches and for
backstitching in green. For the more delicate
backstitched features, use only one thread. When
complete, steam press on the wrong side.

MOUNTING AND ASSEMBLY

For the frame, use a soft pencil to mark the position
of the aperture which will display your photograph or
picture. Cut this out, using a sharp craft knife. Iron
the interfacing to the back of the embroidered
perforated paper, and then use the craft knife to trim
the backed perforated paper to fit your chosen frame,
and to remove the interfacing from the aperture.
Insert the embroidered paper into your frame.

For the trinket box, iron the interfacing to the
back of the embroidery. Take the acetate inset from
the lid of your bowl and place it over the embroidery.
This will enable you to centre the motif within the
circular space available. Using the acetate as a
template, draw around it with a soft pencil. Cut
around the circle with a sharp pair of scissors, and
follow the manufacturer's instructions to complete
the assembly.

WATER VOLE BOX ▼			
(Arvicola terrestris)	DMC	ANCHOR	MADEIRA
⊠ Black	310	403	Black
⊡ Dark brown	3021	382	1904
③ Cream	3047	886	2205
ℕ Deep pink	3607	87	0708
⊥ Dusky pink	224	893	0813
↖ Dark green	3362	862	1601
→ Green	3363	861	1602
▮▮ Brown	610	889	2106
⊡ Fawn	612	832	2108
· Pink	3608	86	0709
■ Pale pink	3609	85	0710
Ecru*	Ecru	926	Ecru

Note: bks the vole's whiskers in dark brown; the eye highlight in ecru*
(*used for backstitching only); the flower stalk and sepals in green;
the vole's front in brown; the vole's ear in cream, and the eye outline
in black.

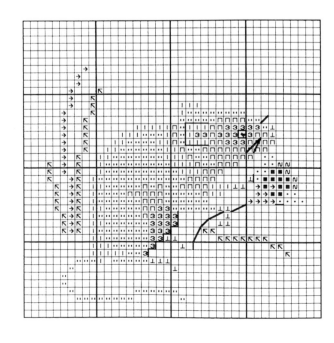

WATER VOLE ▲	DMC	ANCHOR	MADEIRA
⃟ Black	310	403	Black
⊟ Ecru	Ecru	926	Ecru
⊺ Dark brown	3021	382	1904
③ Cream	3047	886	2205
ℕ Deep pink	3607	87	0708
⊥ Dusky pink	224	893	0813
↖ Dark green	3362	862	1601
→ Green	3363	861	1602
↑ Light green	3364	260	1603
❙❙ Brown	610	889	2106
⊓ Fawn	612	832	2108
· Pink	3608	86	0709
■ Pale pink	3609	85	0710

Note: bks the vole's whiskers and the flower stamens in dark brown; the vole's eye highlight in ecru; the flower stalks and sepals in green; the vole's front in brown; the vole's ear in cream, and the eye outline in black.

Mallards
Tea Cosy

Fresh white provides the perfect
background for the wild irises and
pond, on which swim a striking
mallard and his mate. The scene is
a restful design for the tea table, but
could equally well be set into a
small tray or framed as a picture.

MALLARDS TEA COSY

YOU WILL NEED

For the Mallards Tea Cosy, measuring
30.5cm × 24cm (12in × 9½in):

40cm × 36cm (16in × 14in) of white,
14-count Aida fabric
36cm × 30.5cm (14in × 12in) of white
Aida or similar fabric, for back of tea cosy
Two 36cm × 30.5cm (14in × 12in) pieces of white,
cotton fabric, for inner lining
Two 36cm × 30.5cm (14in × 12in) pieces of polyester
batting/wadding
Stranded embroidery cotton in the colours given
in the panel
No24 tapestry needle
1m (1¼yd) of No2 piping cord
Matching sewing thread

•

THE EMBROIDERY

Prepare the Aida fabric and stretch it in a frame as
explained on page 5; find the centre by folding, and
mark the horizontal and vertical centre lines with
basting stitches in a light-coloured thread. Set the
fabric in a frame and count out from the centre to
start stitching at a convenient point. Complete
the cross stitching, using two strands of thread in
the needle. Remove the embroidery from the
frame. Leaving the basting stitches in place, gently
handwash the finished piece, if necessary,
and press with a steam iron on the wrong side.

MAKING THE TEA COSY

Scale up the template for the tea cosy shape and
make a paper pattern. Using the basting stitches as
guidelines to make sure that the embroidery is
centred, draw the outline on the back of the Aida
fabric with a well-sharpened hard lead pencil. Cut
out, adding a 12mm (½in) seam allowance all around
the marked shape. Repeat with the backing fabric
and the two pieces of lining fabric. Cut two shapes
from batting/wadding, this time without adding the
seam allowance.

Remove the basting stitches from the
embroidered piece and, with right sides together and
taking a 12mm (½in) seam allowance, join the cosy
back and front together around the long curved
seam. For each lining section, lay the corresponding

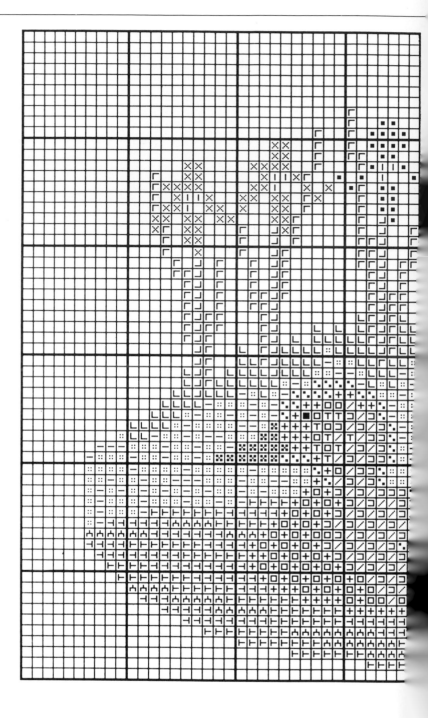

batting/wadding piece on the wrong side, within
the marked outline, and machine stitch the two
together, making three vertical lines of stitches,
one up the centre, and one at each side, 10cm (4in)
from the centre line. With right sides together and
taking the 12mm (½in) seam allowance, join the
padded lining pieces together around the long
curved seam.

Turn the outer cover right side out and slipstitch
piping along the curved seam, from the lower raw
edge at one side to the lower raw edge at the other
side, making a loop at the top of the cosy. Bring the
lower, straight edge of the lining over, covering the
edge of batting/wadding, and turn under the lower
straight edge of the outer cover. Fit the lining into the
outer cover and slipstitch around the bottom edge.

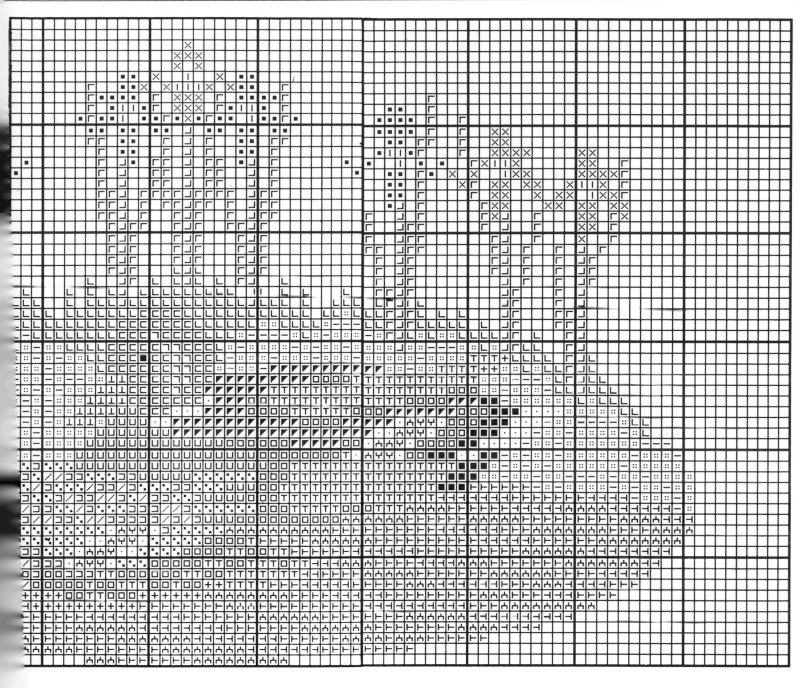

◀ **Tea cosy template**
Scale up by 148 per cent on a
photocopier and cut from folded paper.

MALLARDS ▲	ANCHOR	DMC	MADEIRA			ANCHOR	DMC	MADEIRA
⅃ Dark sand	373	729	2209	• White		1	White	White
+ Stone	831	3782	1907	⊠ Golden brown		365	780	2214
T Greyish stone	392	642	1906	⬚ Pinky brown		832	3032	2002
⊢ Pale blue	130	799	0910	⊥ Straw		874	834	2204
⊿ Medium blue	977	826	1012	⊣ Bright blue		121	793	0906
■ Purple	109	210	0802	Ψ Dark blue		922	930	1712
⎸ Yellow	297	725	0108	⊠ Dark purple		111	208	0804
∷ Olive green	844	581	1609	− Pale olive green		842	772	1604
⅃ Bright green	266	3347	1408	L Grass green		265	471	1501
⌐ Blue green	876	503	1702	⌐ Rich green		267	3346	1407
■ Black	403	310	Black	⊏ Pine green		878	561	1205
⊔ Bright brown	357	975	2302	∴ Dark brown		889	3790	2106
◿ Dull brown	898	370	2112	◤ Very dark brown		382	3371	2004

Bell Pull and Bookmark

In the tall damp grasses alongside a river, the frog finds food and shelter. The damselfly also frequents the area, while in spring the mayfly emerges from the water.

BELL PULL AND BOOKMARK

YOU WILL NEED

For the Frog Bell Pull, measuring 29cm × 10cm (11½in × 4in):

*43cm × 23cm (17in × 9in) of cream,
18-count Aida fabric
35.5cm × 15cm (14in × 6in) of cream lining fabric
29cm × 10cm (11½in × 4in) of iron-on interfacing
Stranded embroidery cotton and blending filament
in the colours given in the appropriate panel
No26 tapestry needle
Pair of metal bell pull hangers, 10cm (4in) wide*

For the Frog Bookmark, measuring 23cm × 7.5cm (9in × 3in):

*26cm × 11.5cm (10¼in × 4½in) of white,
14-count perforated paper
26cm × 11.5cm (10¼in × 4½in) of iron-on interfacing
45.5cm (18in) of green ribbon, 12mm (½in) wide
Stranded embroidery cotton and blending filaments
in the colours given in the appropriate panel
No24 tapestry needle*

•

THE EMBROIDERY

For the bell pull design, prepare the fabric by marking the centre lines with basting stitches. Begin stitching from the centre point on the design. Use two strands of cotton in the needle for all cross stitches, except where metallic thread is indicated. In this case, combine one strand of cotton with one strand of blending filament. For backstitching, use two strands of cotton, except for the detail on the insects' wings, where only one thread is used. Be particularly careful when backstitching over the wings, as it is very easy to catch and snag the metallic thread when bringing the needle through from the back of the fabric.

For the bookmark design, find the centre of the perforated paper by counting the spaces between the holes. Work the cross stitches first, using three strands of thread in the needle, except where metallic thread is indicated. In this case, combine two strands of cotton with one strand of blending filament. For the backstitching, use two strands of cotton in the needle, except for the detail on the insects' wings, where only one thread is used.

FINISHING THE BELL PULL

Centre the interfacing on the back of the embroidery and pin it in place. Remove the basting stitches and iron the interfacing into position. Trim the long edges until the piece measures 13cm (5in) wide. Turn in the long edges by 12mm (½in) and press. Trim the short edges until the piece measures 38cm (15in) long. On the two short edges, make a 6mm (¼in) turning. Make a second turning 4cm (1½in) deep, taking the fabric over a rod at the top and bottom. Baste and neatly hem in place.

Turn in the long edges of the lining fabric and then the short edges, so that it will neatly cover the back of the work. Slipstitch in place.

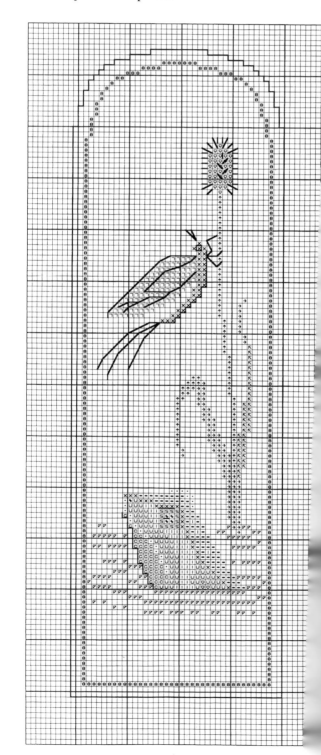

**COMMON FROG, COMMON BLUE DAMSELFLY &
MAYFLY BELL PULL ▶**

(Rana temporaria, Enallagma cyathigerum & Rhithrogena)

		DMC	ANCHOR	MADEIRA
Z	Black	310	403	Black
⊐	Silvery grey	415	398	1803
	+ *Kr. 001 (Kreinik silver blending filament)*			
I	Dark brown	3371	382	2004
5	Gold	972	298	0107
⊡	Light iridescent blue	775	128	1001
	+ *Kr. 001 (Kreinik silver blending filament)*			
·	Blue	597	168	1110
▬	Medium brown	610	889	2106
U	Fawn	612	832	2108
⊼	Dark green	3345	268	1406
→	Green	3347	266	1408
↑	Pale green	3348	265	1409
C	Cream	739	885	2014
◫	Yellow brown	830	277	2114
T	Brown	3031	905	2003
X	Yellow	676	891	2208
I	Yellow green	734	279	1610
▼	Biscuit	738	942	2013
	Grey*	414	400	1801
	White*	White	1	White

Note: bks the frog's back leg in brown; the frog's throat and belly, and the mayfly's body and tail in fawn; the insects' wings in grey; the line over the frogs eye in dark brown; the insects' legs and antennae in black, and the frog's eye highlight in white* (*used for backstitch only).*

OMMON FROG & DAMSELFLY BOOKMARK ◀

	DMC	ANCHOR	MADEIRA
Black	310	403	Black
Silvery grey	415	398	1803
+ *Kr. 001 (Kreinik silver blending filament)*			
Dark brown	3371	382	2004
Gold	972	298	0107
Iridescent blue	518	168	1106
+ *Kr. 094 (Kreinik blue blending filament)*			
Light iridescent blue	775	128	1001
+ *Kr. 001 (Kreinik silver blending filament)*			
Medium brown	610	889	2106
Fawn	612	832	2108
Dark green	3345	268	1406
Green	3347	266	1408
Pale green	3348	265	1409
Cream	739	885	2014
Yellow brown	830	277	2114
Brown	3031	905	2003
Yellow	676	891	2208
White*	White	1	White
Grey*	414	400	1801

e: bks the seed on the reed seed head in brown; the frog's eye light in white; the frog's throat and the mayfly's body and in fawn; the mayfly's wings in grey* (*used for backstitch only); line over the frog's eye in dark brown; and the mayfly's legs antennae in black.*

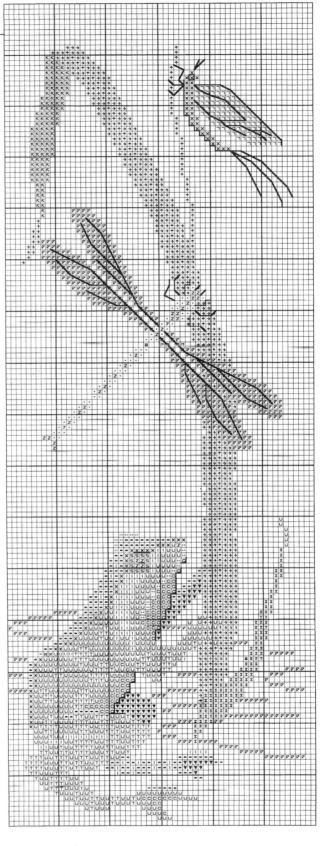

FINISHING THE BOOKMARK

Centre the interfacing on the wrong side of the bookmark, then iron it in place. Trim around the border of the design, leaving an edging of two perforations. You may find it easier to mark your cutting line with a soft pencil before you start. Cut the ribbon in half. Gather along the edge of one piece and tighten it into a rosette. Fold the other length in half to make two streamers, and stitch the fold to the lower edge of the bookmark. Glue or stitch the rosette in place over the streamers.

INDEX

SUPPLIERS

The following mail order companies have supplied some of the basic items needed for making up the projects in this book:

Framecraft Miniatures Limited
372/376 Summer Lane
Hockley
Birmingham, B19 3QA
England
Telephone: 0121 359 4442

Addresses for Framecraft stockists worldwide
Ireland Needlecraft Pty Ltd
2-4 Keppel Drive
Hallam, Victoria 3803
Australia

Danish Art Needlework
PO Box 442, Lethbridge
Alberta T1J 3Z1
Canada

Sanyei Imports
PO Box 5, Hashima Shi
Gifu 501-62
Japan

The Embroidery Shop
286 Queen Street
Masterton
New Zealand

Anne Brinkley Designs Inc.
246 Walnut Street
Newton
Mass. 02160
USA

S A Threads and Cottons Ltd.
43 Somerset Road
Cape Town
South Africa

Fabric Flair Limited
The Old Brewery
The Close
Warminster
Wiltshire
BA12 9AL

For information on your nearest stockist of embroidery cotton, contact the following:

DMC (also distributors of Zweigart fabrics)
UK
DMC Creative World Limited
62 Pullman Road, Wigston
Leicester, LE8 2DY
Telephone: 0116 2811040

USA
The DMC Corporation
Port Kearney Bld.
10 South Kearney
N.J. 07032-0650
Telephone: 201 589 0606

AUSTRALIA
DMC Needlecraft Pty
P.O. Box 317
Earlswood 2206
NSW 2204
Telephone: 02599 3088

COATS AND ANCHOR
(also distributors of Kreinik blending filament)
UK
Coats Paton Crafts
McMullen Road, Darlington
Co. Durham DL1 1YQ
Telephone: 01325 381010

USA
Coats & Clark
P.O. Box 27067
Dept CO1
Greenville
SC 29616
Telephone: 803 234 0103

MADEIRA
UK
Madeira Threads (UK) Limited
Thirsk Industrial Park
York Road,
Thirsk
N. Yorkshire, YO7 3BX
Telephone: 01845 524880

USA
Madeira Marketing Limited
600 East 9th Street
Michigan City
IN 46360
Telephone: 219 873 1000

AUSTRALIA
Penguin Threads Pty Limited
25-27 Izett Street
Prahran
Victoria 3181
Telephone: 03529 4400